D0368937

ISRAEL: A READER

ISRAEL

A Reader – Edited by Bill Adler

Portrait of a Nation and its People

CHILTON BOOK COMPANY PHILADELPHIA NEW YORK LONDON

 Published in Philadelphia by Chilton Book Company and simultaneously in Ontario, Canada, by Thomas Nelson & Sons, Ltd. Library of Congress Catalog Card Number: 68-58350. Manufactured in the United States of America by Vail-Ballou Press, Inc., Binghamton, N.Y. Designed by JoAnn Randel.

CONTENTS

Introduction ❧ *vii*

1 *The Story of Israel* ❧ *xii*
MEYER LEVIN

2 *The Immigrant Ship Exodus* ❧ *20*
GOLDA MEIR

3 *The Deed* ❧ *28*
GEROLD FRANK

4 *I Discover Israel* ❧ *44*
ROBERT GRAVES

5 *Israel and Germany* ❧ *66*
DAVID BEN-GURION

6 *Israel on the Eve of Eichmann's Trial* ❧ *78*
FLORA LEWIS

7 *Israel: Land of Unlimited Impossibilities* ❧ *90*
BARBARA W. TUCHMAN

8 *The Problems of Religion* 118
TERENCE PRITTIE

9 *In the Footsteps of the Past* 134
AUBREY MENEN

10 *Israel: A Nation Too Young to Die* 146
JAMES A. MICHENER

11 *O Jerusalem* 168
MAX LERNER

12 *Israel: The Next Twenty Years* 172
J. ROBERT MOSKIN

INTRODUCTION

If you look at a map of the world and Israel's relative size in it, it hardly seems possible that so much fuss could be made over something so small. Yet, what are the expressions: "A small dog often has a very loud bark" and "You don't need a large box for a jewel"? In any case, the analogies are clear. Israel has made itself heard and, in the twenty years of its existence, has turned its 8,000 square miles into an emerald green oasis in an otherwise agriculturally unproductive and overpopulated area of the world.

As editors, we tried to be fair in the selection of material for this anthology. We tried to find unbiased material, for to be perfectly honest, when a Jew writes about Israel, he is apt to be slightly prejudiced. Yet, opinion seems to be almost unanimous—while Israel certainly has problems to contend with, there is no doubt that its viable existence is a tribute to the men and women who returned to recreate the Jewish state after nearly two thousand years. Nevertheless, hate literature about Israel does exist, not surprisingly from Arab sources, but as is usual with this sort of thing, it is rather poorly written and repetitious.

While gathering material for this anthology, we did, of course, have other criteria in mind. Readability was one; in other words, out of the enormous volume of writings on Israel, we were determined only to select those articles or chapters which were extremely well written. In addition, it was our intention to cover as wide a range of topics concerning Israel as possible. Thus, while Robert Graves gives us a picturesque tour of the country and a marvelous description of the people, Barbara Tuchman offers a comprehensive idea of the problems Israel has faced and overcome, and Robert Moskin speculates on how Israel might come to grips with the problems for which it has yet to find solutions. Flora Lewis, on the other hand, wonders whether the "final solution" has been or should be buried with Adolf Eichmann, or whether it is up to Israel to prod the world's memory.

Ephraim Kishon injects a note of humor into an otherwise serious group of articles, and the book would not be complete without it, for despite everything, the Jewish people have always been able to take themselves with the proverbial grain of salt—although in Mrs. Lot's case, it was disastrous.

There is fiction and history, and frustration and humor in this anthology, for the story of Israel is all of these and more.

BILL ADLER
1968

"Israel is a going concern—something the world must recognize. But one Hebrew told me, 'We've never had security since the age of Solomon.' I told him, 'You're doing fine without it!'"

ROBERT FROST

ISRAEL: A READER

THE STORY OF ISRAEL

MEYER LEVIN

The Middle East, it seems, has always been in a state of turmoil and unrest. The area, Israel included, has been fought over time and time again from the days of Abraham to the present. In an unusually interesting and concise chapter, Meyer Levin traces the history of the Holy Land over the last four thousand years.

Modern Israel and Biblical Israel, though twenty centuries apart, are continuous in the minds of the Jews. Israel is the only country to which, after an interval of nearly twenty centuries, a people has returned.

The country is so small that on an ordinary globe its printed name sticks out into the sea. Israel today is hardly more than a sliver of seashore so narrow in the middle that the entire country can be crossed by car in less than twenty minutes. At its widest, from the Mediterranean to the Dead Sea, Israel is hardly an hour across.

The Bible, of course, makes us familiar with the name of every village and every stream. Indeed, names from this land have been repeated in America: we have a Bethlehem in Pennsylvania and a Jericho in Kentucky, and scores of other such reminders of the Holy Land, which through the Scriptures, projects itself so vitally into the rest of the world.

In Israel itself, many Biblical names remain, others are revived, and many a village carries its legends not only from

Meyer Levin. *The Story of Israel.* New York: G. P. Putnam Sons, 1966.

Biblical times, but from modern times. Driving to a settlement called Gath to show our children where Goliath fell before David, we are reminded by the settlers that this is also where the last pocket of Egyptian forces surrendered in 1948.

In this tiny country you can see nomadic shepherds living in black tents as in Abraham's time, and you can see helicopters flying over the tents. You can see an atomic reactor standing in Yavneh, the site of an ancient Talmudic academy.

Though it is fabled as a land of milk and honey, half of Israel is barren desert; much of the rest is rocky hillside. Why have conquerors and would-be conquerors from Nebuchadnezzar to Napoleon to Nasser dragged their troops and their war engines across this arid earth?

A glance at the globe makes plain that this country forms a land bridge between east and west. If you want to go from Asia or Arabia to Africa without putting to sea, you must pass across this coastal path. If a trader with his caravan, in ancient days, wanted to proceed from Persia to Egypt without encountering the Red Sea, he had to come down along the Mediterranean beaches and make his way over the sands that are now cut by the Suez canal.

Yet, not all the wars over this area have been fought for the control of commercial and military routes or for earthly power. As many have been fought for religious causes.

Besides being the natural corridor between Orient and Occident, the tiny land of Israel has been a spiritual center for mankind. Its capital, Jerusalem, is a holy city for Jews, Christians and Moslems. The Jewish and Christian faiths were born here.

Gradually, from Jerusalem, the divine truth of the brotherhood of man has spread over the earth. Perhaps it was because they saw so much of bloodshed in this place that the Hebrew prophets cried out for brotherhood and for peace. And doubtless, too, they were inspired, for many people going up to Jerusalem have experienced an exaltation that seems to be in the very air. Some believe, quite mystically, that even the quality of the landscape in Israel brings religious inspiration. For it is a landscape both awesome and tender.

Lying among the northern hills is the Sea of Galilee, called Kinnereth in Hebrew because it is shaped like a harp, called a "kinor." The sea is so limpid and peaceful that it is linked forever in our minds to Christian prayers of quietude and love. And yet, from this same gentle sea, the waters of the River Jordan course downward between the stark cliffs of a geological fissure to the sulphurous Dead Sea, covering the buried ruins of Sodom, the Biblical city of wickedness which was destroyed during the time of Abraham. Among the jagged salt pillars that ring the sea, it is easy to imagine the petrified figure of Lot's wife, as she turns back, in the Biblical account, to look at the burning city of evil. Even today, we have no scientific explanation for the cataclysm that destroyed Sodom.

We do know that some gigantic upheaval split the face of the earth long ago, so that the Jordan winds downward far below sea level to the deepest hole on the globe, the Dead Sea, which lies there like an open wound.

Around the Dead Sea rise weird, gray cones as in some imaginary landscape of the moon. The air is torrid, hard to breathe. Acrid minerals are concentrated in the rocks and in the water. It is no wonder that tales of sin and hell originated here, and yet the waters have been found curative, and from the Dead Sea, in a vast engineering project, phosphates are extracted to fertilize the earth.

Thus, in the tiny area of Israel, the extremes of life and death lie before one. The lyrical waters of Galilee plunge to the sulphurous sea, but from there the hills leap upward to a shining city on a rocky height, Jerusalem. In the high place of Jerusalem, the very air, heady and clear, seems to sing to the inner spirit.

Who would want to possess so strange a land? A people of extreme temperament who would love it fiercely. And the story of Israel is the story of a people and a place united, separated, again and again. In their times of absence from each other, the people suffered and the land suffered, but always, in their times of reunion, the people and the land flourished together.

No drama of lovers torn apart and reunited is more romantic than the story of this people and its homeland. The lovers are put through the tests of war, hunger, pestilence, and exile; they undergo the seductions of lavish wealth and pleasure; yet, they remain faithful in their longing for each other, ceaselessly trying to bring about the reunion that has come at last.

When this land first came into history, it was known as the land of Canaan; since then, this land has been called Judea, and Palestine, and now, a part of it is called Israel, a part is called Jordan.

Ancient Canaan was not a "nation" as we know the term today—a unified people living under a single government. The area was inhabited by clans and tribes often at war with each other. Here and there stood small walled cities, each with its overlord or king who ruled a tribe or group of tribes spread out in the surrounding area. Subtribes of the Canaanites were called by the many names that have come down to us in the Bible—the Amalekites, the Jebusites, and the like.

Around the fortified towns were settled cultivated areas, reaching away into open grazing lands, used, according to custom, by one wandering tribe or another, and subject to raids by tribes that had no fixed area of their own.

Herdsmen changed their pastures as the weather changed. This may be seen even today in Israel; in a year of severe drought, when there is no forage whatever for the Bedouin herds in the Negev, the flocks of black goats, sheep, and camels will suddenly appear along the main automobile roads, moving up north. Small though the country may be, it has an extreme variation of rainfall so that twenty miles may make a difference between good pasture and desert.

The Bedouins in Israel appear indeed as an ever-present past, an image of Biblical days. The story is told of one shepherd who, quite impervious to traffic, led his flock straight into the middle of Tel Aviv where they settled down to graze on the lawn of the symphony hall.

It was a shepherd of far earlier times, named Abraham (Kindhearted Father), who led his tribe into this land of Canaan in search of good pasture and of a spiritual home.

He came, over four thousand years ago, from the city of Ur, which has been excavated in modern times, in the country now known as Iraq. The Bible, in many instances proven to be a good history, tells us that Abraham left Ur to seek a land where he could worship in his own way. This is humanity's first recorded quest for freedom of religion.

It was a quest made by a people who seem in any case to have been strangers to the idol-worshiping cult practiced in Ur. For Abraham's people had come down to Ur from the northern mountains. This might well be the region of Mount Ararat, where Noah's ark came to rest. These wanderers must have brought with them certain beliefs of their own, reaching back to the story of Creation, and the Garden of Eden, and then the flood. In the Jewish Talmud, which enlarges on the Bible, we are told that Abraham revolted against the religion of Ur and smashed the idols.

Then he heard the voice of God telling him, "Get thee out of thy country, and from thy kindred, and from thy father's house, unto a land that I will show thee: And I will make thee a great nation."

And so he started off with his household, to seek a land where he could worship in his own way. He crossed the great river, the Euphrates, and trekked with his family and his flocks through the arid wilderness. When he came out of the desert stretches to the green expanse of Canaan, he felt with an ecstasy of pent-up longing that this was his promised land. Again, he heard the voice of the Lord, the invisible God, whom he began to understand as universal. And so, into the soul of this unique man there came the inspiration that marks the beginning of our western civilization, our understanding of the universe. For all around him, Abraham had seen only the worship of idols: idols of the sun god and the moon goddess, idols for every purpose, for having children, and for good crops, for luck and for health. He had seen special gods for clans and for households. He had seen gods whose favor was supposed to be won by human sacrifice.

Abraham himself was tempted, for how could one man so easily shake off all the beliefs among which he had been raised? He still did not know whether this invisible, universal God whose presence he felt was not also his particular tribal god whose name was so powerful that it must not be uttered aloud: Yaweh. Abraham was even tempted later in life, as we know by the profound story of the near sacrifice of Isaac, to place his own son on the sacrificial altar. Yet, in a world of superstition and magic, he clung to the great revelation that there was One God over all life, and that no idol could represent God.

For the sake of this tremendous insight he had become a wanderer. And when he came to the land of Canaan, he recognized the promise of the Lord: "Unto thy seed I will give this land."

Up and down the land Abraham wandered, to settle finally around the place of the Seven Wells—in Hebrew, Beersheba—the site of today's modern city on the edge of the southern wasteland called the Negev. There his children and his grandchildren grew up.

His son Isaac was the father of twins, Jacob and Esau, and Jacob had twelve sons, each of whom became the head of a tribe. Jacob was later called Israel—The Man Who Has Seen God—in memory of a night of mysterious wrestling with a stranger. Thus, the twelve tribes of his sons were the tribes of Israel.

Israel's progeny became a numerous clan; they were called the Habiru, or Hebrews, "the people from over there." A period of drought and famine drove them across the Negev and across Sinai, along the caravan route to the watered lands of the Nile in Egypt. The wondrous tale arose of how one of the sons, Joseph, had foreseen the bad drought, and become the Pharaoh's minister, and laid up stores for the bad years, saving Egypt and saving his own people, too. Thus, his people lived in Egypt for many generations, and under many pharaohs, until there came a pharaoh who "knew not Joseph," and who made slaves of the Hebrews.

Over four hundred years had passed. Then, around 1300 B.C., a great leader appeared, named Moses, who conceived of leading the Hebrew slaves out of Egypt, back to Canaan, to freedom in their own land.

This might be called the first Zionist movement.

But the exodus led by Moses was also, like the trek made by Abraham, an inspired movement in search of God. For, in the Sinai desert, Moses brought to his people the word of God in the Ten Commandments. This was a tremendous moment in the history of man, for here a group of people decided to live by law, taking to themselves by common consent a code of conduct whose great moral precepts have served as the foundation of modern civilization. Under these laws all men were equally bound.

When the Hebrews, after forty years of preparation, came to enter their ancient homeland, they attacked some of the walled towns that belonged to various kings. Under Joshua, they won Jericho and other cities. The twelve Hebrew tribes spread out and settled in different areas, but as the generations passed, the ties between the tribes grew weaker. They were ruled by Judges, or wise men; some, like Samson, being perhaps stronger than they were wise. But the laws of Moses, and the belief in a single God, still gave them a sense of unity.

After some two hundred years, with constant skirmishes and warfare with other people in the land, there arose a

Judge who had great spiritual authority, Samuel. He decided it would be best for the tribes if they were again to combine and fight as one people, to have a king. He selected a stalwart farmer, Saul.

Along the seacoast at this time there lived a people called the Pleshtim, or Philistines (hence, Palestine). Like the Hebrews, they were migrants; the Philistines, however, had come by sea—perhaps as refugees from wars on other Mediterranean coasts. We still know little about this ancient people, though present-day excavations in Ashdod on the Israel coast are beginning to give us a picture of their way of life.

The Philistines had built six towns along the coast, and from these they kept pushing up into the hills where the Hebrews lived. They defeated Saul. He was succeeded by the popular hero, David, who built his fort high on the mountain fastness of Jerusalem. King David drove the Philistines back down to the seashore lands, and brought away the Ark of the Ten Commandments, which they had captured. So, around the year 1000 B.C., came the golden age of the Jewish kingdom.

David was followed on the throne by his son, King Solomon. It was Solomon who built the First Temple in Jerusalem; he made the city splendid, and developed the land. Copper mines were worked in the Negev; ships were sent trading down the Red Sea as far as the domain of the Queen of Sheba, in the region of Yemen today.

After Solomon's death, his heirs fell to quarreling, and soon the country was split in two. The northern part, from the Haifa region to Galilee, was called Israel, while the southern area, around Jerusalem, was called Judea. And so down to our times we speak rather interchangeably of the Israelites and the Jews.

Just when the Hebrews were split and weakened, there came new wars between the large nations on either side of them. The Assyrians marched through Palestine to attack

Egypt. On the way, they conquered the ten northern tribes, called Israel, and drove the people off into exile. From this, we have the legends of the Ten Lost Tribes.

Through the centuries, tales have come of the descendants of the Ten Lost Tribes being found in Russia, in China, even in Ireland. When Columbus discovered America, it was said that the American Indians were the Ten Lost Tribes. But the ten tribes of Israel must have melted in among the Assyrians; if not, they must have been destroyed. In any case, they vanished, around 700 B.C.

All that remained then to the Hebrews was Judea, the area around Jerusalem inhabited by the tribes of Judah and Benjamin. For another hundred years, this little kingdom held out between the Egyptians and the Assyrians.

But then, over the Assyrians, there arose the Babylonians. And in 586 B.C., the Babylonian king, Nebuchadnezzar, carried off the people of the last two tribes into exile.

The fortress-city of Jerusalem was destroyed; the Temple was demolished. In far-off Babylon the captives built a settlement. They were not enslaved and were able to develop towns and even study centers where their ancient Mosaic laws were written down and taught. But they were in exile nevertheless, and they sang a haunting song that has come to be the song of all the heartsick and homesick and lonely, of all the earth's displaced persons.

> By the rivers of Babylon, there we sat down;
> yea, we wept, when we remembered Zion.
> How shall we sing the Lord's song in a strange land?
> If I forget thee, O Jerusalem, may my right hand wither.

And this cry has resounded through the ages.

In only fifty years, this time, the fate of the Hebrews again swung over. Their conqueror was conquered. The new ruler, Cyrus, a Persian, was surprisingly wise for his time.

Finding the Hebrews to be a minority folk in Babylon, Cyrus told them they could go home and live in their own land, rebuild their Temple, and worship as they pleased—provided only that they remain his loyal subjects and pay tribute and taxes from Jerusalem.

Some fifty thousand Jews made the long voyage homeward beginning in 537 B.C. By 515 B.C. they had built the Second Temple.

Not all the Jews left Babylonia. Just as there are Jews today who are long established in various lands and feel patriotic about those lands, there were in those days Jews who had established themselves in Babylon. Indeed, a huge colony was to live on and flourish there right up to modern times.

In their homeland, meanwhile, the returned Jews lived on for two centuries as a Persian colony, until the Persians were conquered by a Greek, Alexander the Great. Palestine was taken over by him in 332 B.C. The worship at the Temple was not disturbed, and the Jews continued as a tribute-paying people until, when nearly another two centuries had passed, there came a Greek ruler named Antiochus.

Antiochus forbade the Jews to practice their religion. In their Temple of the Invisible God, where idols were taboo, he placed a statue of Zeus. He forbade their rite of circumcision, the original covenant of Abraham with his God.

For freedom of religion, the Jews went to war.

A priest named Mattathias and his five sons organized bands of fighters who set up camps in the wooded hills and in caves. One of the five brothers, Judah, led his men in night raids, and because of his smashing blows against the enemy, Judah became known as the Hammerer—Maccabee.

To stop the Maccabees, huge armies were sent in from Syria by Antiochus, but time and again they were caught in narrow passes in commando-like assaults and destroyed. Finally, Jerusalem was freed of foreign rule, the Temple defiled by Zeus was cleansed, and in 142 B.C. the nation was restored to self-rule with the family of the Maccabees, known as the Hasmoneans, as king-priests.

But just as King Solomon's sons had quarreled and split the first Jewish kingdom, so the descendants of the Hasmoneans, in fighting among themselves, threw the second Jewish kingdom open to foreign rule. They had lasted little more than a century.

By then, the Romans had pushed aside the Greeks, the Syrians, and the Egyptians and become the strongest power in the Mediterranean. A Roman general was called in by one side in the Hasmonean family squabble to help gain control of Jerusalem, and from 64 B.C., the Romans took control, making their puppet, Herod, King of Judea in 37 B.C.

Roman taxes were heavy. Life was hard. Hotheaded Jewish patriots kept stirring up nationalistic revolt. A secret terrorist organization, called the "Sicarii," was composed of zealots who carried daggers under their cloaks and stabbed Roman officers and tax collectors. The Romans replied by executing Jewish patriots, when they caught them, as common criminals; the method was to nail a man up on a cross in a public place.

We can understand something of the violence and confusion of those days through recent times, when Palestine was under British colonial rule, and terrorists and counterterrorists kept the country in a constant state of eruption. Like the Sicarii of Roman times, secret members of the Stern group struck down officials of the colonial government, while members of the Irgun dynamited police and army installations, and members of the Haganah carried on widespread resistance actions.

In Roman times too, there were various secret groups, some violently resistant and some, like the Essenes, going off to live a life of purity. Today, the amazing archaeological discoveries of the Dead Sea Scrolls are giving us new insights into the atmosphere in the Holy Land in those days and into the life of groups like the Essenes, whose settlements in some ways resembled monasteries and in other ways resembled kibbutzsim.

It was during this dreadfully troubled period that the Jews began to speak more and more longingly of the coming of the Messiah, a leader who would bring peace and spiritual perfection to the world. How the Jewish idea of the Messiah first began is not yet clear to scholars; perhaps, it had in it a longing for a leader like Moses. And to the austere area where the Jordan cut down to the Dead Sea, an area in which there was a settlement of the Essenes, there came a prophet-like preacher, John the Baptist, who purified people in the Jordan river and who is said to have proclaimed the coming of the Messiah.

It was during this period that a young Jewish preacher from Nazareth began to stir men with his message of brotherhood. His name was Joshua, or Jesus, and He was said to have been baptized by John and to have known the Essenes. Many of His teachings were close to those of the revered Rabbi Hillel of the same period, others went further than the ideas of Hillel in their attacks on the rich and powerful. Accounts spread of the miraculous healing powers of Jesus, and He went through the towns of Galilee. He was attracting a huge following.

It is not difficult to understand, then, in those times of unrest, that the tumultuous popular acclaim of Jesus should have troubled those in the seats of power, both Jewish and Roman. Among the Jews, power was in the hands of the rich and influential families that controlled the priesthood in Jerusalem. In general, they were collaborators with the Romans. They were worried over the growing popularity of this preacher from Nazareth and worried too over teachings that they sincerely believed to be in violation of religious laws.

Among the Romans, it was feared that the crowds aroused by this preacher might in reality represent an underground resistance movement that could be turned into an upheaval for national liberty.

At the height of His popularity, Jesus, with a number of His followers, came to Jerusalem for the Passover. He demanded reforms in the Temple, cleaning it of commercialism and money-changers. The High Priest was alarmed and had Him seized for questioning. Then, the Gospels tell us, He was turned over to the Roman governor, Pontius Pilate, who questioned Him, found He had violated no law, but on the demand of the High Priest's faction, had Jesus crucified. Yet, he had a sign affixed to the cross—King of the Jews—which would indicate that the Roman indeed held Jesus to be a leader of a nationalist movement. And we are told that instead of Jesus, Pilate released a man named Barabbas, a patriot who had killed someone—perhaps Barabbas was an underground fighter whom the Jews wanted freed.

So Jesus came to be crucified in a way which was later to be blamed on all the Jews, forever, though it is clear that Jesus and His followers were themselves Jews and that those who declared He was the Messiah were Jews. In recent times, the Catholic Church in Rome has declared that it is wrong to blame the Jews, as a group, for the death of Jesus. Through the centuries, this mistaken teaching had caused untold grief and hatred in the form of anti-Semitism.

The believers in Jesus as the Messiah first preached to fellow Jews, so that the first Christians were pious Jews within the synagogue. Later, they preached their belief abroad to the Gentiles, and eventually the Christian religion took hold in Europe and became a great world movement.

In our time, the close link in the moral teachings of Judaism and Christianity is seen in the wide use of the term "Judaeo-Christian civilization."

In those ancient years of the birth of Christianity, the Jews, who as a whole did not believe and have not believed that the Messiah appeared, continued their struggle against the Romans in their land. For another few decades the

Romans kept them under control. But thirty years after the time of Jesus, the Roman governor looted the Temple treasury and interfered in Jewish worship. Just as they had revolted against the defilement of their Temple by the Greeks, the Jews now tried to revolt against the Romans.

This time, however, there was no Judah the Maccabee to unify them. The Romans sent a powerful army to besiege Jerusalem, where leaders of the uprising had taken positions behind the strong walls of the Temple area. Now, the Romans built their own barrier, a stockade outside the city walls, so that no supplies could get in. The starving Jerusalemites fought among themselves, and finally, in 70 A.D., the city fell.

Thousands of Jews were crucified. Others were sold as slaves or dragged off to be exhibited and torn to pieces in Roman arenas. Large numbers of refugees fled across the desert, some eastward to Babylonia, some southward to Egypt. Still others sailed to all corners of the Mediterranean sea. The typical Jew became the wanderer.

A few last-ditch fighters held out in caves near the Dead Sea. The last of their strongholds proved to be the rock fortress of Masada, a sheer cube-like formation looming above the sea, on which Herod had built a palace. The Romans encircled Masada in an attempt to starve out the unyielding Jews. For two years the siege continued. But at last, after the Romans had built a huge ramp to the top of Masada and begun to batter down its walls, the Jews saw that their plight was hopeless. With their wives and children, they were less than a thousand in number. They decided on mass suicide rather than to live without freedom.

Yet, after the revolt had been completely subdued, some numbers of Jews lived on in the villages. Their rabbis established hidden schools and academies for the study of the Torah. And after another seventy years, a warrior named Bar Kochba, with the sanction of the great Rabbi Akiba, led the last nationalist uprising against the Romans.

When Rabbi Akiba declared that Bar Kochba was the

Messiah, the Jews flocked to the fighter's standards. Half a million fell. Rabbi Akiba was captured and tortured to death. This time the Romans decided to erase even the memory of Judea; they changed the name of the land to Syria Philistina and so came "Palestine."

The holy city of Jerusalem was razed and plowed over, and Jews were forbidden on pain of death to set foot in the Roman city that was built on the site. This city was named after a Roman emperor, Aelius, and in Aelia Capitolina, temples were built to Bacchus and Venus.

Darkness fell over the land.

But as the decades and centuries passed, the Jews in their village academies kept on with the study of their laws, slowly compiling the great body of wisdom, tradition, parable, and law known as the Talmud.

The Jews who lived in Babylon were doing the same. Contact grew, as scholars were exchanged between the two communities, but to this day both the Babylonian Talmud and the Jerusalem Talmud are studied.

In some villages in Palestine, such as Peki'in in upper Galilee, a few Jewish families persisted with their lineage intact down to our own times, to be rediscovered by early Zionists at the turn of the century.

The Roman Empire declined after some centuries, and in the deserts of Arabia a new religion arose. Mohammed knew many tales from the Hebrew Bible, and he knew of Christianity, for he adopted the Jewish prophets, as well as Christ, in his Koran. He knew of Jerusalem as a holy place, for he related a dream in which he ascended to heaven from Jerusalem.

In the sixth century, Mohammed's followers, spreading the Moslem religion with the sword, swept out of the Arabian desert and conquered a large part of the Mediterranean world. Jerusalem was theirs. Where Solomon's Temple long ago had stood, they built the Mosque of Omar in memory of Mohammed's dream.

For the next five centuries, the Moslems ruled.

But the Christians of Europe were aroused at the idea that the Holy Land was ruled by Moslems. The Crusades began. King Richard the Lionhearted of England was one of those who carried the Christian banner across the Mediterranean sea to storm Jerusalem.

For a hundred years the Crusaders held sway from forts built at strategic points, such as the ancient Roman port of Caesarea. But then the Crusaders were in turn conquered by savage troops from the eastern realm of Saladin. Again and again the Holy Land was drenched in blood, until it was captured by the Ottomans, and from 1516 Palestine was ruled from Turkey.

As the forests were cut down for fuel, the hills became bare; the topsoil, washed away by the winter torrents, left only rocks. The downpour cut gulleys through the lowlands; plains became swamps, and swarms of mosquitos spread malaria. The Valley of Jezreel—the vale of Israel—became known as the Valley of Death.

Still more wars were to come. In 1798, Napoleon Bonaparte, striking from Egypt across the classic highway of the Holy Land, attempted to pierce the Ottoman Empire. Napoleon called upon the Jews of the world to join him, promising them the return of their ancient homeland. But before they could answer his call, Napoleon ran into a sudden defeat at Acre and promptly scuttled back to France.

And so the ancient land lay in decay, an aggregation of sickly villages, with Jerusalem hardly more than a small town, and the whole country ruled by a governor appointed —usually for a price—by the Sultan in Turkey.

Over the centuries, in the waves of conquering armies, there had come wandering tribes from among the desert Bedouin, who had taken land and settled here and there. It is even believed by some scholars that, in the mud-hut villages whose way of life remained unchanged from Abraham's time, clans lived who were descended from the original Canaanites.

And what of the Jews in all this time? Scattered over the

world, they had built communities in Spain, France, England, Germany, Poland, Russia, America. Again and again they had been driven from their communities or slaughtered.

At the time of the Crusades, they had been expelled from England and from France and slaughtered in pogroms by Crusaders passing along the Rhine. In 1492, under the Inquisition, those who refused to become Christians had been driven from Spain. Then, and at other periods, numbers of Jews had returned to the ancient homeland.

Sometimes in flight, sometimes inflamed by the urgings of some self-appointed Messiah, the Jews through the centuries had established communities of the pious in the Holy Land. In certain cities, such as in Hebron where Abraham had bought a family burial cave, they had established rabbinical schools. In the hill town of Safed, where the great rabbis, hiding from the Romans, had conducted their secret academies in the caves, there had grown up groups of mystics who wanted to be near the tombs of the sainted religious leaders.

These mystics believed they could decipher the secrets of the future and of the coming of the Messiah, through codes that they applied to the Holy Writings. Every letter of the Hebrew alphabet is also a number and, by combining the numbers that belonged to the first letters of the words in certain Biblical passages, they believed they deciphered profound secrets. Those initiated into this mystic lore were called Cabalists, from the Hebrew word "qābal," which means to receive.

There were Cabalists in Jerusalem, too, and Talmudists who pored over the vast stream of rabbinical writings, many still seeking for hints of the time when the Messiah would arrive on his white mount, to enter the Holy City and bring His reign of peace upon the world.

And there were the simple, pious Jews who came, somehow, from all corners of the world, to live out their last days and die in Jerusalem.

In some way, despite pogroms, inquisitions, expulsions,

burnings, and butcherings, the Jews kept their faith and their identity. Their faith was strong enough to enable them to clutch the tail of another cyclone of history and ride that cyclone through two world wars back to their homeland.

In all the turmoil of argument about the rights to Palestine, one thing is to be noted: not in all the centuries when the land was governed by Romans, Greeks, Crusaders, Moslems, Turks, never in all history had any people who lived in the land, except the Jews, tried to set up their own government.

When the Hebrews first appeared, Canaan was a land of scattered warlords each ruling the immediate area around his city-fort. Egypt was then already a nation; Assyria was a nation. Palestine was a place, a passage between these two countries. No people living in Palestine had ever unified the area.

In the high period of King David and King Solomon, unity was achieved. But after the Jewish kingdom was destroyed, rebuilt, and again destroyed, Palestine fell under a succession of foreign rulers—Romans, Saracens, Ottomans. During all these centuries, the inhabitants of the Holy Land never became a nation.

Only with the return of the Jews in this century was this to happen.

THE IMMIGRANT SHIP EXODUS

GOLDA MEIR

Under the British mandate of Palestine, Jewish immigration into that country was severely thwarted. Fearing Arab reprisals, the British continually turned back the European Jews who had endured so much suffering during the war. The Exodus *arrived in Palestine waters in July, 1947, and despite pleas from around the world, despite a series of hunger strikes and resulting sickness aboard ship, the British refused entry to the vessel's 4,000 passengers. The ship was sent to France, where the passengers would not disembark. They were then transferred to three other British vessels and ultimately sent to Hamburg, Germany, where they were forcibly ejected from the ships and sent to displaced person camps.*

The truth is that there is practically nothing left to say on the episode of this ship, an episode that symbolizes in the most striking manner not only the situation of the Jewish people but also the condition the whole world is in today. The things that have happened in recent weeks, ever since the Exodus reached the shores of this country—and even before that, when she was still outside Palestine territorial waters—and that have gone on happening up to this very day, could not have happened were it not that even now, after the victory over Hitler, the world is still living very largely in the same atmosphere that he created even before the outbreak of war and during the war itself. Perhaps, the most disturbing, the most shocking thing of all, is not what happened to the few thousands of people on this ship, not what happened to babies, pregnant women, to old people and to youngsters; what is most shocking is the fact that not a single country, not a single person almost, has been found to cry out in

Golda Meir. "The Immigrant Ship Exodus," *This Is Our Strength.* New York: Macmillan Co., 1962.

bitter protest against this wrong. We have yet to hear of anyone besides Jews who have volunteered to fast along with us.[1] It is true that every one of us knows very well that in this world of ours a fast by Jews is not likely to move anyone, but it would have been fitting if at least some few Gentiles somewhere in the world had fasted along with us—not for our sake, but for the sake of the conscience of humanity and for their own conscience's sake.

We know that on this ship there are scores of women who are about to give birth or who have just given birth. Babies have been born on this ship. Where are the women's organizations of the world that fight for women's rights, for equality and justice for women—where are they all? Why aren't their voices raised against this injustice? And it is in this world that we have to fight for the minimum of justice that is our due. I doubt whether any other people would have the courage to go on fighting in conditions like these and in the face of forces like these. Maybe if the Jewish people had any alternative, they too would have despaired. But since they have no other alternative, and since they are convinced that justice is on their side, and since they are convinced that if they want to go on existing as a people, then this is the only course open to them—they are fighting on in spite of everything. And strange as it may seem in the eyes of outsiders, in spite of everything, the Jewish people are sure that victory will finally be theirs.

In our present circumstances, let us survey—for ourselves and for others—some details of this struggle.

The British Government will not succeed in blurring over the clear fact, the primary, fundamental fact, that the ship was attacked and people on board were killed while she was outside Palestine territorial waters. The British Government is trying to prove—and is obliged to try and prove—that this is not so, but they have not yet succeeded in doing so. They have not succeeded and they will not succeed be-

1. Jewish Agency leaders and other national figures undertook a joint fast in protest against the British deportations of "Illegal immigrants."

cause the facts in our possession all prove the contrary, that is to say, that the ship was attacked on the high seas in contravention of international law. She was attacked with considerable force, and it is a miracle that she succeeded as she did in reaching the shores of this country.

This ancient people of ours has an excellent memory; it forgets nothing: it does not forget the good that has been dealt us and it also remembers the evil. And exactly as we shall never forget what the British Government is doing to us now at this juncture, even so, we shall never forget the noble stand taken on this issue by the Government and the people of France. This must certainly have been a bitter disappointment for Britain.

From the day the Exodus reached the shores of this country, all our exertions were unavailing—everything that was done by the Jewish Agency, the Jewish National Council and the entire Jewish community in this country, as well as by Jewish bodies that were active in London, in other European countries, and in Washington—until the day came when the British issued this communiqué of theirs announcing that they were returning the immigrants of the Exodus to Germany, this communiqué full of the wicked and baseless accusations without a shred of truth in them, that we have heard so often in recent years.

There is something bigger and stronger than the threats of the British, and that something is the will to live of the Jewish mothers who bore their babies on the ship, Jewish women who had decided in their hearts that they wanted to be free in their own homeland and that they would not leave the ship anywhere else in the world. Against this will of theirs even the British Government is weak; they can kill mother and child, but this will to live they cannot kill. As long as there is still one Jew alive in the world who wants to come and live in the Land of Israel, the British Government will have to use force if they want to stop him.

According to this communiqué of theirs, the Jews really want to go to Germany, for have they not been given the alternative of landing in France? And if they don't want to land in France, that clearly proves that they want to go to Germany! And the communiqué goes on to say: if the Jewish Agency is really concerned over the well-being of these Jews, let them send an emissary in all haste to explain to them that they should take advantage of the favor that the British Government is doing them, and that they should come down off the ship and go into exile once more.

This communiqué gives the reason why the British Government has stopped sending Jews who are trying to come in here to the camps in Cyprus—because this maneuver has failed. Even after they knew that they would be deported to Cyprus, the Jews kept on coming, and the British now hope that by means of this battle on the Exodus they'll finally succeed in frightening off the Jews of the DP camps and us here in this country. To this, there needs be only one answer: the streams of Jews coming here in these ships will not stop! I have no doubt nor fear concerning the stand of the Jews of the DP camps; they are ready to leave the camps at any moment. Their leaving depends only on us Jews, on each and every one of us, wherever we may be—and if we here and the Jews of America and South Africa and England don't panic, if we will only understand what is behind this battle, then the ships will keep on coming in.

There's something else we have to point out to the British Government. In the Special Assembly of the United Nations called to discuss the Palestine question, a resolution was proposed by the representative of Norway and passed by the Assembly calling on all governmental and non-governmental bodies inside Palestine and outside it not to resort to the use of force or to threats of force during the period of the deliberations of the U. N. Special Commission on Palestine. And we now ask Great Britain and the United Nations who it was that acted against this resolution. When the resolution was passed, what was the situation? Ships were coming here carrying Jews determined to enter this country. The British Government didn't agree to it. And we didn't agree that these ships should be turned back and sent off to Cyprus. But there was nothing new in the fact that immigrant ships were reaching this country. Who changed the position that prevailed at the time that this resolution was passed? Who started the use of force, and by so doing, tried to alter the status quo existing at the time of the U. N. investigations? We say that it is the British Government that is guilty of a gross and open breach of the United Nations resolution. When the U. N. General Assembly reconvenes in September, it will be incumbent on it to put on record what has happened in the period since the Special Assembly on Palestine, to put on record whether it is the organized Jewish community in this country that has done anything to disturb the peace and to cause fresh trouble, whether it is the Jews of the camps that are doing anything, or whether it is the British Government. We want to have weighed in the balance the British Government on the one hand and the Jewish community here on the other. Which of them broke this U. N. resolution, which of them wants to face the United Nations Organization not only with threats to use force but with the actual use of force itself—shooting and murder?

And since we may not despair, we want yet once more to send out an appeal from here to the nations and to the world, to those nations many of whose citizens suffered no little during the war, to those for whom Jews fought on many fronts in order to help liberate them. We turn to these nations and to these peoples and we make a last-minute appeal; is it possible that not one will lift up its voice, that no one will say to the British Government, "Drop the whip and the gun, leave these Jews in peace!"? And to England, let it be said, "You are mistaken if you think that we are as weak as all that." Let Great Britain with her splendid navy and all her guns and planes know that our people is not so weak—it will yet find the strength within itself to fight this battle too!

But the main thing concerns ourselves, the Jews; the

main thing is the need for maximum mobilization on an unprecedented scale in order to infuse the whole community with the determination to have no part in furthering the British Government's designs. And to have no part doesn't only mean not sending an emissary to coax the Jews to leave the Exodus—that's not enough. Having no part in the British Government's designs in its war against the Jews means mobilizing all our strength in order to smash the law that forbids Jews to enter the Land of Israel. And to those who will say mockingly that every appeal in this country ends up with a demand for money, let me say, "Friends, every Jew in this country and every Jew in the Diaspora, rich and poor alike, every Jew, as a Jew, must be rich enough to do his share in bringing Jews alive to the Land of Israel." And to all those in whose power it is to help Jews reach this country in every possible way, let us say from here, "Blessings be upon you!" Pure and holy are these youths from the Land of Israel, from America, from every country, every Jewish youth who risks his life in order to bring in a mother with her baby, in order to bring in a Jew to the Land of Israel. Pure and holy are they, our pride and joy. And those of us who are not privileged to carry out this sacred precept in our own persons can help carry it out by providing the means. We can and must meet the demands made on us. Let Britain know that each and every one of us will certainly do what is demanded of him, and if she knows this, perhaps she will think again. And if she does not do so, she will have to face this people of ours as it is today—in the camps, in Cyprus, in this country, in America—everywhere that there are Jews, she will be faced with these Jews who will know one thing, that their lives depend on Jews entering the Land of Israel. And since it all depends finally only on us ourselves, on our strength of will—and since we have no alternative—they will keep on coming, and they will enter the Land.

THE DEED

GEROLD FRANK

The Deed *is the true story of the assassination in Cairo during World War II of Lord Moyne, the British Minister of State in the Middle East, by two young Jewish boys, Eliahu Bet Zouri and Eliahu Hakim. The boys were members of the Jewish underground terrorist organization and were subsequently hanged for the murder.*

The following selection takes place during their trial in Cairo, at which time they try to explain the motivation for their deed.

It was Bet Zouri's day in court—the day of his speech.

The news had spread. It was impossible to obtain tickets for the trial.

Bet Zouri stood in the dock, his arms folded across his chest, facing the President. He was dressed as before—a gray sweater over his open-necked shirt—and his casual, almost collegiate appearance was in sharp contrast to the deadly seriousness of the moment. He began to speak quietly—his face pale but composed—and to our astonishment, he spoke in English. The interpreters are "unable to translate my Hebrew as faithfully as I would wish," he explained, "and my Arabic, I regret, is not good enough. So I shall address you in English and I hope everyone will bear with my mistakes."

I was seated next to Fred Lee, the American Broadcasting Company correspondent. We looked at each other. Bet Zouri was making sure that we—the American and British correspondents—would understand, would miss no word. Through us, he would speak to the world.

Gerold Frank. *The Deed.* New York: Simon & Schuster, Inc., 1963.

Bet Zouri told how he and Hakim met, how they followed Lord Moyne, the photograph they carried, their debate as to where to carry out the deed. They agreed that Hakim would fire at Moyne because his revolver had a simpler mechanism than Bet Zouri's and rarely jammed. "It is the kind of a pistol known as a six-shooter and is very popular with American cowboys," Bet Zouri explained gravely. There was stifled laughter and the President sounded his gavel sternly. "But if my comrade failed in the attempt, we agreed that I would shoot the lord." Again he said, "We are not interested in killing anyone." Their idea was to force everyone but Moyne out of the car and make them lie face down on the ground. By isolating Moyne, there would be no chance of hurting anyone else in the action. "However, we forgot to think that anyone would attempt to stop us. That is our fault. Nobody in the world is sorrier for the death of the driver than ourselves."

He was completely at ease now. There was no sound in the courtroom. He spoke slowly, carefully, as if to miss no point nor exaggerate any. His arms were no longer folded across his chest; now he leaned forward, one foot on his chair, his right elbow resting on his right knee, his left hand on his left hip, like a seminar instructor explaining a subject to a small group of students. He made few gestures. Hakim sat behind him, listening intently, now and then glancing over the audience as if trying to read their faces.

Bet Zouri told how the limousine rolled up to the gate, how he and Hakim ran toward the car:

"But when we were near it, we saw that the captain had already gotten out and also the driver. My comrade was busy; as the driver came toward the car, I pointed my gun at him. He was a meter away. I told him, 'Stop. Lie down!' He did not reply but came nearer me. I ordered him again, 'Lie down!' Instead, he raised his hand to catch my revolver and I pulled the trigger. I remember exactly that when my brain gave the order to my finger to pull the trigger, it was not to kill him but to prevent him from snatching my revolver."

Speaking reflectively, almost as though thinking aloud, Bet Zouri went on:

"I have asked myself many times since, if I did not mean to kill Fuller, why did I fire three times at him? I have not been able to find a satisfactory answer. I cannot say that I lost my mind. I was quite cold-blooded and remember very well that, when I pulled the trigger, I counted one, two, three." He paused for a moment. "It seems that the answer is that it was habit. When members of our organization train in Palestine, we are accustomed to fire three times to see how well we concentrate our bullets on the target. I repeat that I did not mean to kill Fuller, who was engaged in a war that had nothing to do with our war, and I regret it more than I can say."

He described how he and Hakim raced to their bicycles, how they were trapped on the bridge, how he was seized after an exchange of shots. Now he grew indignant. "I disagree with the court on the charge that I tried to kill the constable. The reason I fired at his tires was because I did not want to hurt him." And now he became doubly indignant. "It is not true that I tried to kill him but failed because I am not a good shot. When he caught up with us, it would have been easy to kill him at a distance of six meters. If you do not believe what I am telling you, it can very easily be proved." He leaned forward, resting his elbow in the space between two palings, gazing directly at the President. "If the court will place a revolver into my hand . . ." He raised his voice above the sudden hum of astonished amusement—"if the court will give me a gun, I promise to put six bullets . . ." He paused, and his eyes met those of the President directly in front of him. He stretched forth his arm as though his hand held a revolver and pointed it at the President. "I will promise to put six bullets into the face . . ." Pause again. ". . . of that clock . . . above your head."

It was done dramatically and effectively. The audience chuckled. President Mansour Bey grinned almost sheepishly. The Public Prosecutor lost his gaunt, sad look for a moment and smiled; catching the President's attention, he tapped his own chest as if to say, "They would be happy to place the bullets here, too." The President composed his face, turned to Bet Zouri and said gravely, "That will not be necessary." He rapped his gavel. "Will you continue, please."

Bet Zouri brought forth from his pocket a few sheets of penciled notes. He placed his foot on the chair and began, almost formally: "I shall now explain to you the reasons that caused me to act as I did."

The room was very still.

"For this purpose I must go back a few years to a scene I saw when I was a boy in Tel Aviv. I remember standing on the balcony of my father's apartment and watching many people gather in the street. It was an interesting sight for a boy of twelve or thirteen—this large crowd of grownups shouting, carrying flags and so on. Grownups standing near me said, 'This is a demonstration.' As I watched, I saw police, among them British police, come in from the surrounding streets with sticks and stop the demonstration. It was a little strange. I knew then that an English policeman is a man coming from England to be a policeman in my country. And when I saw one of the policemen bring his stick down on the head of a demonstrator, I asked myself, 'Why should a man leave his home and family in a far-off country and come three thousand miles to my country to be a policeman? Why can this Englishman hit my people and they cannot strike back?"

Again there was a rustling as Egyptian turned to Egyptian with knowing smiles. Not only Prime Minister Ahmed Maher himself had been involved in the Black Hand terrorist organization, but even some of the members of the court had been nationalist terrorists in their student days. Hassan Djeddaoui, who had been the first of the defense counsel to visit Bet Zouri in his cell, had written an autobiographical sketch for the correspondents in which he listed among his achievements a year's prison term for "anti-British activities."

"I did not understand then," went on Bet Zouri, speaking slowly and precisely, "that the English are in my country because of the mandate of the League of Nations. They were given the rule over Palestine because they promised to help build a Jewish National Home. But instead of carrying out this duty entrusted to her, England seeks only to broaden her rule in Palestine. She imposes her . . ."

The President's voice interrupted him acidly. "The accused is making a political speech. If he persists, I must ask all correspondents to cease taking notes. The political aspects of this case are not within the competence of this court."

Commotion in the courtroom. Over the noise, Bet Zouri's voice:

"I am sorry, but I disagree with you. It is not a political speech."

He was standing, arms folded, facing the President.

The latter said, "I am sorry, too, but that is my ruling."

Bet Zouri: "I am making my defense, your Honor, and I must go ahead with it."

The President sounded his gavel. "No report of the proceedings beyond this point is to be published." He ordered the bailiffs to confiscate all writing materials of the correspondents. They would be returned at the close of the day's session. This is incredible, I thought; yet, we witnessed the astonishing spectacle, we participated in it. I watched as the elaborately uniformed guards, each with a revolver conspicuously at his belt, moved among the correspondents representing the press of the world—C. L. Sulzberger of The New York Times, Christopher Lumby of the London Times, Relman Morin of the Associated Press, Walter Collins and Sam Souki of the United Press, Grant Parr of NBC, George Moorad of CBS, the correspondents of Agence France Presse, of Reuter's, of Palestine's Davar and Haaretz, Palestine Post, of all the press and radio networks of the free world. We yielded our notebooks, our sheafs of paper, our pencils and fountain pens, and sat impotent. Bet Zouri calmly resumed his speech, while the guards stalked watchfully up and down the aisles, to see that we did not surreptitiously put down a word he uttered. Bet Zouri and Hakim faced the gallows for killing a man; if they were unable to explain what motivated them, the deed lost its significance—and now we were barred from giving this testament to the world.

"I have studied the British Administration in Palestine," Bet Zouri was saying, and though he faced the President, it seemed that he was directing his words to us; we were the audience, no one else. "I learned that it is full of injustice, graft and anarchy. Every inhabitant is forced to obey the law, but there is no law which the Administration or the police is forced to obey. Injustice, partiality and cruelty prevail everywhere." He gave examples: the administration had compelled all Palestinian citizens to sell to it gold coins at a fixed price; later, the same administration sold the same gold coins back to the citizens at a price four times as high. At the same time, it announced that it was fighting war profiteers. "But when a poor Tel Aviv storekeeper sells merchandise a penny above the set price, he is arrested, fined and jailed for months. Does this law apply to the Administration? No."

Bet Zouri paused. He leaned forward: "I tell you, in Palestine, the Englishman is master. He is a god. His word is the law. All the inhabitants, though they are the natural sons of the land, are natives who must obey the master. This is the consciousness the English seek to plant into the hearts of the peoples of all countries where they rule."

Looking off into the distance, speaking almost regretfully, now and then fingering his mustache as he paused to find the right word, he went on:

"I have never had the chance to visit England—that land whose sons fight all over the world for freedom, that land that is the mother of the Magna Carta, of habeas corpus—so I don't know what the Englishman is like in his own country. But I think that he must be like Doctor Jekyll and Mr. Hyde. In his own country, he is a gentleman of the highest order, but when he goes abroad into the colonies, he becomes something else. He drinks the wine of power and becomes so drunk that he thinks he is the god of the native . . ."

"This is irrelevant!" the President snapped. "I warn you . . ."

Bet Zouri stiffened. "But strangers are doing things in my country as they wish! We can do nothing. They will not listen. What are we to do, to whom will we turn?"

In the silence that followed, he continued in an almost conversational tone. "The situation in Palestine reminds me of a book written by a great writer, Jack London. In *The Sea Wolf,* he tells of a shipwrecked man who is rescued by another ship. He thinks his suffering is ended, but it is only beginning. For the ship that rescues him is a little state with its own laws, and the laws are the muscles of the captain. Everyone on the ship has to obey the orders of this captain. He is autocratic, a cruel man without mercy. No one can dispute his word; the muscles of the captain are the law, and in Palestine, the muscles of the police are the law.

"I tell you that the conduct of the English government in Palestine is worse than that of the cruel captain on the ship. Millions sank in a sea of blood and tears, yet the English captain did not allow them on the ship that could have saved them. He stood on the deck and saw without pity how the people were sinking. If some of the drowning managed to hold on to the sides of the ship, he, the captain, pushed them back into the sea to sink and drown. And we who saw all this with our own eyes had nothing left but to surrender—or fight. We decided to fight—to destroy the foreign ruler, to drive out the cruel dictator . . ."

President (sharply): "Stop this! You are making propaganda! Get down to facts. What has this to do with the killing of Lord Moyne?"

Bet Zouri, suddenly losing his calm as he stood in the prisoners' dock behind the spike-tipped iron staves fencing him off from us, took one step toward his judges, leveled that accusing finger and in a voice so impassioned and carrying the accents of such righteousness that it almost brought us out of our seats, cried, "Our deed stemmed from our motives, and our motives stemmed from our ideals, and if we prove our ideals are right and just, then our deed was right and just!"

Behind me I heard Egyptians say, one to the other, "A strong man! A strong man!" And then a woman's voice, "What a pity that a boy like that was led to do such a terrible thing!"

The President, taken aback, stared at him for a moment, then looked down at his blotter and said, in Arabic, his voice almost gentle, "Continue."

Bet Zouri stepped back. He was composed again. Subtly, in ways difficult to describe, he had the courtroom with him now: President, state prosecutor, clerks and interpreters, the audience, the correspondents. One cannot condone murder. He had committed murder. Yet the courtroom was his.

He continued to speak, turning to us, directing his words to us, the correspondents, as if to say, "If my words will be heard beyond the gallows, it is because one of you will carry them with you from here."

Patiently now, like a schoolmaster: "Some may say we have no right to attack the English because it is thanks to them that we live in Palestine. There is no truth to this argument. We, the Hebrews, the natural sons of the land of Israel, fought for Palestine before the Balfour Declaration. We are the natural and legal owners of the country. We do not recognize England's right to give us Palestine or to take it away from us."

He paused. "Let me make clear to the court. My ideas are not Zionist ideas. We don't fight to uphold the Balfour Declaration. We don't fight for the sake of the National Home. We fight for our freedom. In our country, a foreign power rules. In our country, England is a stranger who does what she wants.

"The crimes she commits are without number. I can give you names, dates, addresses; nothing can refute my accusations. To the English everything is 'the law.' When an English policeman clubs a Hebrew young man in the street in Jerusalem in nineteen thirty-nine and leaves him dead, 'that is the law.' When another English policeman shoots a deaf old man and leaves him dead on the ground, 'that is the law.' When Captain Morton breaks into a house in Tel Aviv and murders Abraham Stern, shooting him in the back, 'that is the law.'

"In Palestine, the Jews are trying so desperately to do wonderful things, but they are blocked and stopped. Young Palestine is full of initiative; its citizens seek its progress. But the English Administration is not ready to hear any suggestions. They will not listen. Whatever they want in our country, 'that is the law.' I wish I could tell you—my English is not good enough to express how badly the Administration rules. It rules with fear and torture. The English torture chambers are always full in Palestine. The CID tortures those who fall into their hands, to get information. They do it scientifically; they know anatomy and the most sensitive parts of the body. They go far beyond what is called in the United States the third degree. I will call witnesses who will tell you the truth of what I say. And when the English arrest and torture, 'that is the law.' "

The President asked, "Was there no other way to protest but by the gun?"

Bet Zouri (hotly): "To whom could we protest? In a country which has a parliament, a cabinet, which has freedom of press and speech, you can protest against injustice, corruption and cruelty. But these freedoms do not exist in Palestine. If we have turned to the gun, it is because we were forced to turn to the gun! When we found every other effort would not help, we understood then that the only way to fight a rule based on violence is to use violence. That is why we decided to fight the English by using their own means, to attack the representative of their government, which is responsible for all our misfortunes."

President: "I warn the accused not to continue on this line . . ."

There was an exchange between them and then Bet Zouri's voice sounded above the other's, loud and emphatic, in words that rang through the court:

"Sir, I am not telling you why we fight, I am telling you why we fight so severely. If you think that what we want is to change a bad government to a good government, you mistake us. What we want is to tear it out by the roots and throw it away!"

It was electrifying. One almost expected some of the audience to break out in cheers.

Over the commotion, the President had to pound his gavel repeatedly. When he spoke, his voice was harsh:

"Accused Bet Zouri, if you have anything else to say pertaining to this trial, say it. Otherwise, stop. We have listened to you now for nearly two hours."

Bet Zouri looked at him. Then, with a gesture almost of disdain, he said dryly, "If the court is tired of hearing my voice, I will retire."

He sat down and folded his arms.

The President had to pound for order again.

"Accused Hakim, do you wish to speak?"

Hakim rose. He spoke in his deep voice, strained, hesitant, and the words, in English, came uncertainly. But there was a brooding power in the simplicity of his speech. "The Bible says, 'Thou shalt not kill.' Why for then did we kill?" There was no other way for them to make the foreign government respect their rights. "If we are asked to answer to the killing of Lord Moyne, we in our turn accuse him and his government of the murder of thousands of our brothers and sisters, of robbing our homeland and our property." He expanded on Bet Zouri's theme. What law was there before which Moyne and his government could be held responsible? To whom could Hakim and his people turn for justice?

"That law—the law of justice—is yet to be written in the law books but it is written in our hearts." He said, his head up now, his shoulders back, his hands still clasped behind him, "In the name of that higher justice we ask the court to declare us innocent and let us go free."

He seemed about to add something to this but Bet Zouri leaned toward him and tugged at his jacket. Hakim sat down, silent.

There was the sound of the gavel. Court was adjourned. Defense counsel would take over on the following day.

I walked out of the courtroom with Relman Morin of the Associated Press. Morin, a dispassionate correspondent, was saying, "When he said, 'If the court is tired of hearing my voice, I will retire,' I wanted to go up and shake his hand. Quite a fellow . . ." We began to talk about the banning of the speech. Others joined us. We all agreed that the President had gone far beyond his authority in ordering us not to take notes. That was a question of censorship and outside his province. I was surprised at my own indignation. "We've got to get that speech down—then see what happens," I said.

In a few minutes we were all in the press room, sending out tortuously phrased dispatches which mentioned Bet Zouri's speech without quoting it or summarizing its contents. The readers of Sulzberger's story in The New York Times read the following report:

"One is permitted to state that Bet Zouri delivered himself of what is permitted to be described only as a 'political tirade.' This 'political tirade' lasted two hours and was coolly and calmly spoken by Bet Zouri in a fluent if frequently slightly incorrect English, so that all the foreign correspondents seeking to report the case could fully understand . . . Bet Zouri's tale was long and dramatic, but the dramatis personae, the sense of individuals or countries, cannot be mentioned. . . . It is permitted to state that Bet Zouri contends that 'the ideas I am going to mention are very different from Zionist ideas.' "

After sending our own cryptic dispatches, we gathered in

an ante-room. We were all incensed. Had any of us managed to take notes? Fred Lee of ABC had scribbled a few key words on his shirt cuff, in the best undercover-agent tradition; I had gotten some words down on a two-inch pad; Collins and Souki had also surreptitiously taken a few notes. I sat down at a typewriter; the others stood about me in a circle and we began to pool our memories to reconstruct the speech of Eliahu Bet Zouri.

Our point was this: If the court wished to keep Bet Zouri's charges confidential, the courtroom should have been cleared save for the opposing attorneys. But at least 300 persons had been in the room. Garbled accounts of his words were already circulating through Cairo. Since all we wrote would go through a panel of British, Egyptian and American censors, political as well as military, we should be allowed to report the speech as a legitimate part of our stories, and then allow the censors to do what they must. Censorship itself was bad enough, but muzzling the news at the very source was an outrage.

I set to work. Everyone wanted a copy of the speech. With an original sheet and six carbons in my typewriter, I began taking dictation alternately from one or the other about me. Generally, we agreed on what had been said. Sometimes we disagreed as to Bet Zouri's exact words, but sentence by sentence, paragraph by paragraph, we resurrected out of the limbo of that courtroom in Cairo the words Bet Zouri had used to explain the deed.

I was busy typing when the door opened and Colonel John V. McCormack, British Press Relations Officer, entered. He looked at us sharply, but went on to his office in an adjoining room. We held a quick council. Some were for telling him; others were against it. Sulzberger said, "I'm going to tell him. Perhaps we can get him to help us get it out." At that moment Colonel McCormack emerged from his room and Sulzberger approached him. We were putting together Bet Zouri's banned speech, he told him; we proposed to incorporate it in our next dispatches. Since military security was not involved, would Colonel McCormack intercede in our behalf with Prime Minister Ahmed Maher?

He refused. If the court had ruled against taking notes, Colonel McCormack did not see that our request came within his province.

Morin spoke up. "We'll ask the Prime Minister ourselves."

I folded the top copy of Bet Zouri's speech and put it in my pocket.

That night a committee of three—Morin of the AP, Souki of the UP, and Sulzberger of The New York Times—called upon Prime Minister Ahmed Maher. The Prime Minister sent out word that he was ill and could not receive them. The committee made an appointment to see him the following day. Again he was unavailable.

The denouement of this incident came a week later, when Major Patrick Welch, Public Relations Officer of the U.S. Army, Middle East, Colonel McCormack's opposite number, called me in.

"I understand that you and several others have been doing something you should not do," he said. "In fact, I think I should inform you that you are under contempt of court for having taken notes on the speech of Bet Zouri."

I could only stare at him.

"You're not the only one," he said, with a smile. "I have just received a letter from Colonel McCormack pointing out what you and the others did. But you're really the one they're after."

"Why me?" I managed to ask.

"Let me read you a line from McCormack's letter," said Welch. "In addition, Mr. Gerold Frank is preparing to fly to New York this weekend and will most likely carry a copy of the speech on his person."

I had planned to return to the States that weekend. I *had* the speech on my person.

I remained in Cairo several weeks longer than I had expected.

In the infirmary at Tel el Kebir camp, where she lay ill of a virus infection, Yaffa Tuvia heard the other ATS girls from Palestine speak bitterly in Hebrew about the two Eliahus. They followed the trial day by day. "Such murders we do not need!" one was saying. She threw down the newspaper. "They are a shame to all of us. The sooner they are hanged, the better!"

Another shook her head. "Do you read how this Bet Zouri talks about himself? No, he is not an ordinary killer—he has a brain, he must wait for his brain to tell his finger to pull the trigger . . ."

They could scarcely contain themselves.

Yaffa had destroyed the few names and addresses of her contacts. Sooner or later, she was sure, she would be arrested. No one could be more thorough than British intelligence. I must be strong, she told herself. She kept silent, and she waited.

I DISCOVER ISRAEL

ROBERT GRAVES

Most of the writers in this anthology are Jewish themselves. Therefore, it is particularly interesting to discover what a non-Jew thinks about Israel. Robert Graves finds the country "exciting" and the people full of "vitality." The following selection is an excellent description of Israel and the Israelis.

"So you are about to visit our country?" asked my friend Arnaldo. He is a stateless Hungarian Jew, formerly a Budapest physician, long forced by circumstances to earn his living as an antique dealer in Spain. Arnaldo calls Israel "our country," though he has never been there, and neither has his Berlin wife, who had her medical career similarly cut short because she was Jewish. And millions of other stay-away Jews throughout the world speak of Israel as "our country."

Why did I go? Because friends had assured me that Israel is the most exciting country to visit in the modern world—they were right—and because I wanted to see for myself how the Jews have adapted themselves to independence after two thousand years of dispersion among usually hostile nations—forced to sing low, smother feelings, pretend the Gentile was invariably right.

Israel is now an island, although her coastline extends for a mere eighty-five miles, as compared with land frontiers of

Robert Graves. "I Discover Israel," *The Mission of Israel.* Ed. by Jacob Baal-Teshuva. New York: Robert Speller & Sons, 1963.

some 450 miles. An island because visitors cannot enter except by sea and air. All road and rail traffic between Israel and her neighbors—Egypt, Jordan, Syria, and Lebanon—has been cut since 1948, when the thirty-year-old British Mandate ended and the Arab-Israeli conflict began. And, although Jehovah's Chosen People have returned to the Promised Land at last, they do not occupy the territories divinely promised them in seven different Old Testament texts. The new Israel is a far longer, narrower stretch of country, containing parts of what was once Philistia, Phoenicia and Edom, but less than half of the Biblical Israel. Indeed, the Jews are securely barred from visiting their holiest national shrines: Bethlehem, the birthplace of King David (as well as Jesus); Old Jerusalem, including the only remnants of King Solomon's Temple—a few courses of its Western Wall—and Hebron, where its tombs of Abraham, Isaac, and Jacob remain under Moslem control. The frontiers, in fact, make neither political nor economic nor ethnological sense. They follow the line of a no man's land that happened to divide Israelis from Arabs one day in the summer of 1948, when an armistice was arranged between them by United Nations officials, whose successors still keep watch on the border zone.

Ever since, the Israelis have wanted a peace treaty; but the Arabs, though suffering most from this stalemate, regard them as usurpers and will not negotiate. The Arabs must find it hard to say "kismet" as they see the wilderness blossoming like a rose across the border, while lying brown, burned, and stony around them.

The Israelis work, as it were, with weapons always at their side, in the manner of Nehemiah's men, back from Babylonian captivity, who rebuilt the walls of Jerusalem. Though unescorted hikes along the borders, especially the Syrian border, are discouraged, there is no nervous wartime atmosphere in Israel nor any lack of luxurious American-style hotels to accommodate holiday makers whose main interests are good food, tranquility, sun, and a wide sandy beach.

What a small island Israel is! A car from Tel Aviv will take you the entire length of the old kingdom from Dan to Beersheba—and back—between breakfast and luncheon. From Lydda airport you can fly across the Negev desert to the Red Sea in an hour.

This year, Tel Aviv, Israel's metropolis, celebrated its golden anniversary. On the walls of the mayor's office hangs an enlarged photograph dated 1909, showing a group of fifty men and women in costumes reminiscent of early Chaplin films clustered on a perfect wasteland and scrub. They are drawing lots of sites in a new township, soon to be founded around a high school. Each ten cents' worth of real estate then bought is now valued at a hundred dollars. Tel Aviv, which already has five hundred thousand inhabitants, will have passed its million mark before many years have elapsed. It has distinctly the look of a southern California city, though without the smog or the press of traffic (even taxis are scarce and behave more like buses, because a city ordinance allows them to be hailed and stopped, even when occupied, by people going in roughly the same direction). In 1909, Tel Aviv formed an insignificant suburb of Jaffa, once Joppa. In 1923, General Allenby opened its main street, which still bears his name. He commented: "A fine street, but where are the houses?" "Come back in ten years," he was told. When he did, he rubbed his eyes.

Despite its glorious past, Jaffa has been swallowed by Tel Aviv. It was the port where Jonah embarked on the voyage that ended in a whale's belly, where Hiram of Tyre sent his loads of cedar logs for Solomon's Temple, where St. Peter was granted his vision of the sheet let down from heaven. And you may still wonder at the offshore rock, crowned with a lighthouse, where, in even remoter days, Andromeda was chained until Perseus killed the sea monster and rescued her.

The mayor, brisk and humorous, wearing the well-pressed suit and highly polished shoes demanded by his office—Israelis are, on the whole, negligent of dress—gave me a gilt anniversary lapel button. It bore the arms of Tel Aviv Jaffa, a lighthouse with seven stars. "Why the stars?" I asked. "One for each of the seven hours which the famous Zionist, Theodor Herzl, recommended as a working day."

During the last few years, Rumania had allowed her unwanted Jews to emigrate, on condition that they surrendered all their worldly possessions in the form of land, houses, money, business, and precious metal, taking with them a maximum of one hundred and fifty pounds of personal belongings. When the Theodor Herzl, our Zim line ship, entered Haifa harbor, the immigrants crowded the gangways, children dancing and singing, older people's eyes glistening with joy and relief at the sight of the Promised Land. Close above the harbor, on the right, towered Mount Carmel, where the prophet Elijah won his contest with the priests of Baal. Buses waited to take the immigrants from the quay to newly built suburbs or country settlements. There, each family would find a temporary home prepared —running water, furniture, bedding, chinaware, linen, food in the larder, a week's wages in advance, and jobs for every one next morning. Once acclimatized, the immigrants would be free to choose a permanent home. A hundred thousand more had been expected this year, but the Rumanian government suddenly cut off the flow. Nevertheless, Rumania was only one source of immigration, and a five per cent increase in Israel's population is probable, even without Rumanians. Whatever strain this may impose on Israel's economy, no Jew will be refused entry, since an article in the constitution welcomes all Jews of whatever race, age, or capacity.

Under the British Mandate, most Jewish settlers spoke English, which is still Israel's second language. Now every one must learn Hebrew. Aged newcomers find the task troublesome and a babel of foreign tongues can be heard in buses, streets, and shops—French among Jews from Morocco, Algeria and Tunis; Yiddish among Eastern Europeans; Arabic among the Iraqi, Egyptian, Syrian and Yemenite immigrants. Also German, Spanish, Italian, Dutch, Persian—even Burmese and Finnish. Children, however, pick up fluent Hebrew within six months of arrival and, as a rule, refuse to speak anything else at home. Nearly all Israelis have chosen Hebrew surnames and the language provides a strong national cement. Yet, from a cultural and economic point of view, it has obvious disadvantages. Thirty years hence, Israelis are unlikely to be speaking and writing English fluently, and the rest of mankind is unlikely to learn Hebrew, with its quaint syntax and a script which, though beautiful, not only runs backward but omits necessary vowels (as someone said: "you have to guess by the context whether a word spells dog, dug, or adagio"). Nor can the many gifted, young Israeli writers, whom I met, expect foreign recognition, and they find it hard to make a living, even in a country that boasts the third highest per capita book consumption in the world. Modern Hebrew contains numerous foreign loan words; for example, any mechanical defect in an automobile is a puncture—spelled solely with consonants, it looks catastrophic. In shops, it was always a guess what alternative language I should have to use—English, French, German (close enough to Yiddish) or Spanish. The best barbers were Persian Jews from Bukhara, but signs and grunts got me a very effective haircut.

Among the more picturesque of recent immigrants are the fifty thousand Yemenites from southern Arabia, conversation with whom proved quite beyond my powers. They claim to have left Judea in 586 B.C., when King Nebuchadnezzar sacked Jerusalem. Wealthy and influential in the Yemen for over a thousand years, they had long since been degraded to serfs by Moslem oppressors. A Yemenite Jew riding an ass was forced by law to dismount on meeting an

Arab of even moderate rank and formally offer him the beast. His house roof might not top those of his Arab neighbors. If he died before his children came of age, they were seized and converted to Islam. Yet, the Yemenite Jews remained serene in their faith, trusting the Divine promise of an eventual return to Jerusalem. The women, many of whom are skilled silversmiths, love brilliantly colored dresses and have features and figures that put most European beauties to shame; the men carry themselves nobly and are known for their uprightness. All seem overjoyed by the miraculous fulfillment of a prophecy that sustained them throughout their exile. Isaiah had written: "They that wait upon the Lord shall renew their strength; they shall mount up with wings as eagles." In 1950, when the Yemenite vanguard suddenly crowded into the British Aden Protectorate on hearing that Israel was a nation again, the Jewish Agency chartered a fleet of four-engined passenger planes to ferry them home. This eagle flight, since it had been foretold, did not disconcert the Yemenites, but the huge buses which met their planes at Lydda terrified them. Eagles were in order; no one was expecting dragons!

A color bar never vexed ancient Israel, doubtless because Moses married a black wife and struck his sister Miriam with leprosy when she objected. Hence a group of black Falasha Jews from Ethiopia were given a warm welcome. These trace their descent to King Solomon's guards, some of whom escorted the Queen of Sheba back after her stay at Jerusalem and settled in the Ethiopian mountains.

A desolate coastal plain, north of Tel Aviv, lacked only water to revive its ancient fertility, and the Israelis solved this by sinking artesian wells. The plain of Jezreel, where once the River Kishon formed vast malarial marshes, was drained and now raises wheat and alfalfa. Boulder-strewn hillsides of Judea and Galilee, which hitherto supported a few goats and camels only, called for bulldozers, swarms of workers to heap the stones into walls, and long-distance irrigation; the red soil now supports orchards and vineyards.

I had an unforgettable view of northern Israel from the summit of Mount Tabor, where the prophetess Deborah once watched Barak destroy Sisera's Canaanitish army. All around its pine-covered slopes stretched a cultivated plain checkered in black and green. Far off to the north shone the snows of Mount Hermon; eastward lay the Sea of Galilee and the Jordan Valley; westward the Mediterranean; southward Megiddo, where King Solomon's stables had recently been excavated, Mount Gilboa, where King Saul committed suicide after his defeat by the Philistines, and Naboth's vineyard, which once again yields enviable grapes.

Among the glaring white immigrant villages and towns that have sprung up from one end of Israel to the other, I came across a few well weathered, comfortable settlements dating from the last century. Only Pequi'in, a small Galilean limestone village—original and authentic—has remained obstinately Jewish since before the Christian era, surviving a long succession of wars of persecutions. Non-Jewish communities abound. Arab towns such as Acre continue their accustomed way of life, with turbans, camels, donkeys, mosques, crowded bazaars, and veiled women carrying pitchers on their heads. Whenever I visited a Druze, Kurdish, or Circassian village, it was like crossing a new frontier, and the various monasteries marking Gospel sites proclaim themselves inalienably Italian, German, Russian, French, Spanish, or Greek.

The headman of a Druze village on Mount Carmel, hearing that I was a fellow Christian, consulted me through an interpreter about the local olive orchard, which had borne no fruit for three consecutive years. I found, on examination, that the trees had been sprayed annually by the Ministry of Agriculture. My answer, for what good it might do him, was that they had worked far too zealously—no insects remained to fertilize the blossoms.

Israel's Arabs present a problem. Those who did not

actively resist the Israelis when they seized power in 1948 are treated with all the courtesy the Mosaic law extends to "the stranger within thy gates." But though they may still worship God as they please, though they are undeniably more prosperous than their neighbors who fought, fled, were dispossessed and now languish abroad in resentful poverty, the Israeli Arabs remain an undigested minority. They must have military passes to venture anywhere near a frontier, where the outer ring of settlements is always well armed and wholly Jewish.

Israel wears its friendliest look between the September vintage season and the April wheat harvest. Summer can be devilishly hot. The fresh-water Sea of Galilee, which looks tempting enough on a map, lies 696 feet below sea level, and no cool sea breezes reach it; so the smart Galai Kinereth Hotel at Tiberias, on its western shore, closes from June to September. A traditional Christian pilgrim route takes in the large Capernaum synagogue, where Jesus allegedly read and interpreted the Scriptures; but, though its ruins may overlie an earlier building, they are a couple of centuries too late for authenticity. This road continues to the Hill Beatitudes and a church commemorating Jesus' miracle of the loaves and fishes. Both sites were chosen at random by ancient Byzantine clergy (notorious sellers of fraudulent relics), who also exploited a wrong Cana of Galilee, Jesus' Cana, a site still undisturbed by pilgrims, having stood inconveniently far away.

The lake, at least, is authentic. Tall, melancholy, bearded Mr. Wallisch, head of the fishing industry, might well model for St. Peter, although until Hitler marched into Austria, he was a Viennese tailor.

"Two nights ago," he told me, "the Syrians machine-gunned our boats. No one got hurt, but it disturbed our work."

"How is the fishing?"

"Good. Last Thursday we netted eight and a half tons."

"Tons? The disciples' miraculous catch amounted to a mere hundred and fifty-three fish!"

"Yes, tons. We use echo-sounding equipment, flares, and nylon nets. The government launch protects us. Our catch goes straight from the nets into refrigerators. The clean fish, I mean. Scaleless fish are unclean, and therefore, unsalable. St. Peter's fish fetches a handsome price—you may remember the tax penny found in its mouth—very large, plump and tasty. . . . Yes, there are sudden storms, with waves as high as nine feet. They must have looked dangerous from the apostles' little craft."

A week later, Mr. Wallisch suffered a severe loss: Syrian frogmen, trained in Egypt, cut away his nets.

Nazareth, predominantly Christian and not a very clean town by Israeli standards, lives off the tourist trade and the fame of its ancient churches. Swarms of flies and touts descend on visitors, but fly-switches fail to discourage either. The touts no longer sell pieces of the True Cross, or Noah's Ark, or the Virgin's bed, as in medieval times; instead, you are offered "guaranteed exact copies, duly blessed by the Bishop, of the authentic nails used at Golgotha"; and crucifixes "made of olive wood cut from the two thousand-year-old trees on the Mount of Olives" (although the Mount of Olives has been out of bounds these last ten years). I tried to shake off touts and flies by entering an obviously Jewish bar, but nevertheless found a Christian welcome inside. A "Bethlehem" occupied one corner of the room—a miniature landscape with small painted figures of the Holy Family in the Cave, facing the shepherds, the Three Kings, sheep, camels, asses, Bedouins, olive trees, vineyards, houses, the Inn, all lovingly executed. For the benefit of visiting Protestants, the barkeeper had added a large Christmas tree lit by colored electric candles and a jolly vulgar Santa Claus, enormously taller than either St. Joseph or the Three Kings, his sack spilling toys, dolls, and trumpets.

The kibbutzim, the communal collective settlements, form

the mainstay of Israel's agriculture. There are over two hundred of them, for the most part affiliated to the dominant Mapai, the Labor Party, and run on surprisingly nonreligious lines. Members, in fact, disregard theological dogma and content themselves with practicing love of their neighbors; they seldom possess a synagogue and often break the Sabbath without scruple. Each new kibbutznik adds his or her private fortune, if any, to the common stock and works for the common benefit. Food, clothes, tools, health, services, transport, education, movies, furniture, cigarettes, all come free; the only cash the kibbutznik handles is a small annual allowance for books, records, ornaments or travel expenses on an approved errand. A council, elected by ballot, chooses executive officers and allocates jobs. No ordinary member need worry about taxes, or form filling, or licenses. His house is his own, and when the day's work has ended, he can be as private as he pleases. Children (the kibbutz' greatest treasure) sleep together in Children's Houses, which are also schools, under the charge of trained nurses. After being told bedtimes stories, kissed and tucked in by their parents every night, the children do not see them again until the following afternoon, when they go off and spend three hours at what they cannot quite call "home" because "home" means where one lives and sleeps. This arrangment frees mothers for work. All adults labor indefatigably, goaded by social conscience, from dawn to the children's hour with meal breaks in the communal dining room. No seven-hour day here. As the children grow older, each age group (boys and girls are never separated) moves into a senior house and gets more and more employment in the fields. At eighteen, childhood ends, arms service begins for both sexes, and presently you have a new member demanding a house of his or her own. Kibbutz children tend to be intensely nationalistic, reject rock 'n roll in favor of old-fashioned Israeli round dances, despite city dwellers and mere brain workers. Meat is scarce and expensive in Israel, and the kibbutz meals are temperate and mainly vegetarian. But each Sabbath brings a regular banquet.

The communal system runs efficiently, because it has been chosen rather than imposed. A member may leave whenever he pleases, though in many kibbutzim the original contribution is nonrefundable; he or she draws a single month's subsistence allowance while finding a new job elsewhere. Even so, fellow members usually consider resignation an act of ingratitude bordering on treason; and if two young people from different kibbutzim meet in the army and decide to get married, a lovers' tug-of-war often follows, with each trying to haul the other into his or her own fold.

I gathered that freedom from worries about housing, money, or jobs among people who have grown up in a competitive society leaves many kibbutzniks feeling blank. Natural worries tend to fill the vacuum with fanciful substitutes. And though the money motive is absent, the power motive remains. If ambitious members set their hearts on high council posts, even the solid good will of a sensible majority cannot always control intrigues. A single mischievous and attractive Eve has also been known to demoralize an entire kibbutz. She began by seducing the council member in charge of accommodations and, having won from him a little house at one end of the kibbutz, hooked most of the other council members, too, persuading each of them in turn that he was her only lover. When undeceived, they could not get rid of her without a public scandal, which she herself did nothing to provoke.

My general impression of the kibbutzim matched the late eighteenth century reports by English visitors to the American backwoods: the same hospitality, the same watchful, austere struggle, the same scorn of needless elegance, except that, in general, the American backwoodsmen liked to keep their distance from neighbors, swilled hard liquor, and had souls above art, literature, or music.

Rehovoth, in the orange belt between Tel Aviv and Jerusalem, has claim to be considered the spiritual center of the new Israel. Here Chaim Weizmann, the first President, built himself a beautiful country house. His widow, as it were the Queen Mother of Israel, is in her eighties, though nobody would believe it from her alert mind, active tread, and resonant laugh. Mrs. Weizmann nurses one deep regret; after six gallant attempts she is still unable to learn Hebrew. Constant crowds flock around her husband's monument, and the district has now been proclaimed a national memorial. Another monument to him stands close by: The Weizmann Institute of Science, its departments ranging from nuclear physics to plant genetics. Heavy water and heavy oxygen are manufactured here, and an electronic computer solves problems of appalling difficulty. When I saw this machine, it had just worked for 1,000 consecutive hours, at 20,000 sums a minute, demarking the lines made by helium gas on the spectrum and emitting miles of perforated tape. Only a human brain of extraordinary caliber can feed intelligible questions to a mechanical brain; but in the entrance lobby I saw a young man with luminous eyes and a luxuriant beard, reclining among shelves of multilingual learned papers. He impressed me far more than the monster he served.

Southward, extending about 3,500 square miles, lie the poor lands, the badlands and the howling wilderness known as the Negev. Habitable Israel ends at the boom town of Beersheba. A Bedouin market center, ever since Abraham dug a well there some four thousand years ago, it had grown from 200 to 42,000 inhabitants in ten years. The River Yarkon waters are now piped down to Beersheba, though not in sufficient volume to irrigate all the land under plow. Rain is so scarce—three inches a year—that desert farmers must count on losing one harvest in two; this year's had to be written off.

A broad highway, 150 miles long, links Beersheba with Eilat on the Red Sea. The first stage passes through the wilderness where Hagar, Abraham's discarded concubine, wandered, carrying the infant Ishmael; it ends at the well where she finally relieved her thirst. Ishmael's descendants, Moslem Bedouins who number fifteen thousand, still roam this desert. They pitch and strike their black tents, pasture camels and sheep wherever they can, sow winter wheat in sheltered valleys, and return some months later to harvest it. Every Thursday, a camel fair is held at Beersheba, beginning at dawn and ending by mid-morning. Camels are bought and sold mostly as butcher's meat—Arabs being gluttons for camel stew. Usually sheep are in good supply, but the worst drought for fifty years had killed so many that, when I went to Beersheba, none was on sale. The fair also served as a marriage mart, though the wares are not on show; nor could a non-Moslem like myself have bought a new wife as easily as Mrs. Roosevelt soon afterward bought her granddaughter a young camel. Bride payments for Bedouin girls have risen, in sympathy with the price of other commodities, to about five times the prewar rate. Young men therefore scheme how to import cheaper brides from Jordan. Tribesmen keep secret contact with Jordan by means of dope traffic, difficult to suppress, which passes across the Negev to Egypt, and Colonel Pinhas Amir, the young military governor of the Negev, whom I met at Beersheba, has a hard task in controlling the nineteen different Ishmaelite tribes, some of whose chiefs are now Jordanians.

Until 1948, a local drought did not worry the Bedouins. They could move their flocks west or northwest, as far as Damascus in Syria or Beiruth in the Lebanon; now they are stuck in Israeli territory and must apply for a military pass to graze their depleted herds on waste ground north of Beersheba. Colonel Amir would like them all to settle down in houses supplied by the government. But even a promise of running water cannot tempt them to renounce their limited freedom. They prefer to eke out scanty food supplies by smuggling.

After Hagar's Well, the ferociousness of the desert is

unrelieved. Between Beersheba and Eilat, settlements are few and small. The largest is occupied by Indian Jews, natives of Travancore. Sede Boqer kibbutz has an orchard of peach trees, date palms, and plum trees. A couple of years hence, when water is piped down from the north to supplement existing wells, Sede Boqer, with its good loose soil, may become almost another Beersheba. In 1956, the kibbutz's best-known member, David Ben-Gurion, Premier of Israel, temporarily resigned his appointment and came home; whereupon half of his fellow members moved out, complaining that too many reporters and snoopers were disturbing their tranquil lives. Here I bought a thick handwoven rug of wool locally spun and dyed. I like to think that it came from the sheep that Ben-Gurion himself used to clip.

At the southern end of the Dead Sea, a signpost read, "To Sodom." Our car turned off the highway, and on the sky line appeared a city of flat roofs and an occasional, massive building. But, though solid enough, it proved to be an illusion; those were only cliffs of rock salt, weathered by the wind. No pre-Roman archaeological finds have been made in this area; nor, indeed, are any to be expected, since the Dead Sea shores would have been the world's worst site for a city settlement even of pastoralists. Moreover, "Sodom" and "Gomorrah" are words of execration such as no sane founder could possibly have chosen. Modern Sodom, which consists solely of the Dead Sea Chemical Works, lies nearly thirteen hundred feet below sea level, and workers in its potash and bromine factories cannot long withstand the summer temperature—123 degrees on an average. After brief spells, they must be taken by truck to rest camps on higher ground. It seemed plain to me now that this phantom city, the salt pinnacle of distinctly female appearance which stands gazing toward it, and the hideous heat, gave rise to the Biblical legend of Lot, Lot's wife and the rain of fire.

Lot's sons were Moab and Amnon, and the Sodom legend, which the compiler of Genesis included as a warning against moral perversion, ends with their incestuous birth—useful political propaganda, defaming these idolatrous tribes. My ill opinion of Lot's wife was not improved when, stumbling over her salty skirts, I put a finger out of joint. Another discovery: the "Dead Sea fruit," which the proverb has turning to ashes in the mouth, is real. A plant I found growing in the neighborhood looks like a small watermelon, has similar leaves, ripens to the color of an orange, and keeps its attractive appearance until the sun has dried it to a mere shell which then collapses into dust at a touch.

Near Sodom I saw a herd of fifteen camels, unattended by so much as a dog, crossing the frontier from Jordan; apparently the Jordanian pastures were even poorer than these. After two or three days, I was told, the herd returns. But if a camel were missing, its owner and his kinsmen would invade Israel and avenge themselves on the tribesmen suspected of stealing it.

Forward, through the terrible, tortured desert, a paradise only to the geologist. At one point, a cliff of pre-Cambrian rock rises from an earlier formation, and I could lay my finger on the precise spot where life on this planet began—a thousand million years ago—since no fossils of any sort occur below the pre-Cambrian level. Motor traffic, I found, does not alarm desert gazelle; they enjoy state protection (as also do porcupines) and somehow survive droughts. Wild asses, ostriches, and wild cattle (mistranslated in the Bible as "unicorns") have long become extinct.

Yotvata kibbutz, the first green oasis at the approaches to the Red Sea, supplies Eilat with fresh vegetables, poultry—white Leghorns stand the heat best—and eggs. When I arrived there, a swarm of locusts had just been driven off by the time-honored method of clashing kitchen utensils together; a plane had then pursued the swarm, spraying it from the air. Myriads of prawnlike carcasses littered the desert highway. Half of Yotvata's water supply goes to the copper mines at Timna, which already extract thirty tons of copper a week from the crushed green rock of a tall cliff. Not far off lie King Solomon's copper mines, dating around 1000 B.C. Without sulphuric acid, his miners could not extract copper from rock that had even so high a metallic content as Timna's one and a half per cent. So they tunneled the red sandstone cliff in pursuit of a forty-two per cent lode. Their low galleries, lined with wasps' nests, penetrate deeply into the hillside, and heaps of slag, practically copper-free, mark the ancient kiln sites. Solomon's wealth was based on copper; four ingots could be bartered for one of gold.

Eilat, at the head of the new oil pipeline, and destined to become a large naval base, is also a winter seaside resort, much frequented by skin divers. Here I met Oscar Friedmann, Eilat's oldest resident, a skin-diving pioneer; he has taught many of its most celebrated exponents how to gain the confidence of fish by imitating their behavior. We toured slowly off the coast in a glassbottomed boat, over fantastic groves of coral and fish of every color from canary yellow and scarlet to electric blue. At one point the fish could be seen chasing one another around the mastheads of a sunken fishing vessel. Among the coral lie exotic seashells. I was given a Negro-lipped cowrie, which legend associates with the Queen of Sheba, who landed here on her visit to King Solomon. But soon, Friedmann told me, many acres of this submarine paradise will be grubbed up and replaced by docks.

I flew back to Lydda, the Biblical Lud, birthplace of St. George, who killed the Dragon. The Negev lay below, lion-colored, cruel, boldly sculptured, including a wide stretch of wasteland which even irrigation cannot redeem—there is no soil at all, nor ever has been.

From Lydda, eastward by road over green plains and up oliveclothed hills, to Jerusalem. A well-built but very quiet city. Anyone asking, "Where will I find the Jerusalem night life?" must expect the time-worn answer: "She is down in Tel Aviv this weekend, visiting." The tone is set by the government buildings, not by a chamber of commerce. Students attend the university to learn rather than to take degrees, and the difficulty of satisfying a hunger for knowledge whets it. A formidable influx of immigrants has strained Israel's educational resources almost to the breaking point; all high schools, for example, are on a two-shift basis.

At the department of archaeology I inspected the Dead Sea Scrolls, displayed behind glass in a crowded alcove. Beside them stood the pale brown earthenware jars, not unlike oversized rolling pins, which had protected them so long. When I went to greet Dr. Yigael Yadin, the former chief of staff of the Israeli Army and now lecturer on archaeology at the university, who was supervising the reassembly of manuscript fragments, he joked, "How do you like our scrolls?"

He knew I cannot read even modern Hebrew. I joked back, "One of your scribes had an evil character and evidently hated his job. I'm appalled by his handwriting."

The premier was kind enough to grant me an interview at eleven o'clock; but, knowing how busy he was, I begged instead to accompany him on his usual morning walk around the outskirts of the city. He consented, and his military secretary called for me at 6:15 A.M. Punctually at 6:30 A.M., we set out together along the country roads, while an armed escort followed us. David Ben-Gurion is in his seventies, small, tough, witty, slightly deaf. He was hailed with affectionate respect by all men and women whom we passed on their way to work and cheered by the first shift of boys and girls gathered outside a high school. His main interest, apart from governmental duties, is Greek philosophy; he loves Plato and reads him in the original Greek. So we discussed Plato vigorously and, at one point, paused to shake hands on our shared dislike of his pupil Aristotle. Another unusual bond between us was the Battle of Albuhera, and his eye lighted up when I happened to mention it. During World War I, Ben-Gurion served in the British Army as

Sergeant Green of the Royal Fusiliers, and I served with the Royal Welsh Fusiliers. A century previously, these two regiments had stormed the heights of Albuhera, held by Napoleon's troops and, after the victory, their few unwounded survivors formed a common mess. A tradition then arose and has persisted ever since that no soldier of either regiment can be refused hospitality by the other. Little Sergeant Green, I have been told by members of his platoon—American Zionists, who joined the British Army in a body, with the object of freeing Palestine from Turkish rule—was a terrible one for discipline. Several of them have found places in the Israeli cabinet; Fusiliers stick together, and it is always the sergeant who holds a company together.

The Old City of Jerusalem, where almost everything of religious importance happened—from Johova's blessing of Abraham to King Solomon's building of the Temple, and so on to the Crucifixion and Resurrection of Jesus—lies eastward in Jordan and can be seen through binoculars only. Yet there are a few sacred sites on this side of the barbed wire: John the Baptist's birthplace at Ain Karim; Gehenna, the ancient municipal rubbish dump, a synonym for hell, now littered with rusty tins; the Tomb of David, which though fraud, is at least a thousand-year-old Saracen fraud. One reaches the shrine, where a venerable rabbi officiates among trappings of gold and purple, through a complex of cool rock chambers faced with old blue patterned Islamic tiles. Pious Jews come here either to read the Psalms aloud from their Bibles or to recite them from memory, their eyes ecstatically closed. Northward, across the Jerusalem frontier, lies the Tomb of Samuel. When our guide pointed this out to us, a Baptist minister from one of the Carolinas asked, "Indeed? Was that the First or the Second Samuel?"

Some three thousand ultraorthodox Jews occupy the Meah Shearim quarter—a self-chosen, strongly walled, solidly gated ghetto in pure medieval style. Their main business in life, financially supported by ultraorthodox American

Jews, is studying the Talmud and praying for mankind. No frivolities are on sale in the small shops, and no movie posters or other advertisements deface the blank walls. The men wear sidelocks, full beards, and wide-brimmed black hats; the women shave their heads on marriage and go about in wigs. Little girls must not reveal any more of their bodies than faces and hands; they have thick stockings reaching halfway up the thighs, wrist-length sleeves, and jackets buttoned below the chin, however hot the weather. Meah Shearim Jews will not talk Hebrew, as being too holy for every day use, and prefer Yiddish instead. They even refuse to acknowledge the government of Israel, declaring that the Messiah alone can found a legitimate state, and for Him they have waited patiently these two thousand years. All the intricate niceties of the Mosaic law and its medieval incrustations are observed, and an automobile passing the Meah Shearim gate on Sabbath gets accurately stoned. Householders pay taxes at pistol-point only, and since tax collectors dun them in Hebrew and expect to be answered in Hebrew, delicate situations often develop.

This happens to be a sabbatical year, during which Jews are not supposed to till the soil or even eat annual crops planted by fellow Jews. In the kibbutzim this ban has long become a dead letter, but not at Meah Shearim. The ultra-orthodox who own land content themselves with watering their fruit trees and other permanent crops; and unless they care to live on dried pulse or tinned food, they buy vegetables from Moslems or Christian Arabs. Hydroponics, a method of growing vegetables in water, now eases their problem; no tillage is needed. Of the girls and young men called up for military service, a few misfits gladly respond and thus escape into the free world; the rest offer passive resistance and are soon invalided out.

Israeli civil law is, for the most part, a legacy of the British Mandate, though land laws date back to Turkish times. Rabbinical tradition governs marriage laws and others of a religious nature. An interesting case came into court during my stay. A man named Cohen was prosecuted for disguising his name. Cohens (the word denotes priestly lineage) are forbidden by rabbinical law to marry divorced women. This man had fallen in love with one, and therefore, adopted a non-priestly alias. He got a severe prison sentence.

The Sabbath, being the prescribed day of rest, the day when one studies the Torah at home, public transport services are suspended, though private vehicles go where they please. No match may be struck on a Sabbath; hence NO SMOKING notices appear in the hotels on Friday afternoons. Guests will find hot coffee waiting at the Sabbath breakfast table because the pot has merely been put on an electric stove—which does not count as work. But chocolate is unobtainable because the mixing of milk and chocolate counts as a positive act of cooking, and the cook must be at liberty to study the Torah all day. So must the waiters; guests help themselves from a cold buffet. For piety's sake, an Israeli Sabbath always lasts longer than twenty-four hours. It begins on Friday afternoon as soon as the sun drops behind a hill and ends on Saturday night only when at least three stars are visible in the sky. The Fourth Commandment teaches patience, obedience, and forbearance—but also ingenuity. Cows and goats may be milked on the Sabbath, to ease their discomfort; but the milk so obtained should be let fall on bare rock. Canny farmers, therefore, place a small rock at the bottom of their pail, thus keeping the law, the Sabbath, and the milk.

Bacon is everywhere off the menu because swine were forbidden by Moses as unclean eating. Though no positive injunction prevents anyone from raising and fattening hogs —there was a 30 per cent surplus of vegetables last year—in practice this cannot be done. No municipality, whether Arab or Jewish, will grant a slaughtering license; nor will the government issue an export permit for live beasts.

Even Israeli nursery literature wages war against the

hog: Gub Gub the pig has disappeared from the Hebrew version of Dr. Doolittle; Disney's three little pigs who defy the big bad wolf are three little bears; the Duchess' baby in Alice in Wonderland transmogrifies itself into a little porcupine, not a pigling. And a single official Israeli pig, shown at the Jerusalem zoo, provides a moral object lesson by being kept as filthy as possible. This zoo contains every land animal mentioned in the Old Testament (with relevant quotations printed above their cages), except Behemoth the Elephant. Money is being raised now to buy a Behemoth.

When the menu is handed around in restaurants, the question always comes: "Meat or dairy?" Rabinnical tradition does not allow meat and milk to be served at the same meal. Most Jews assume that the ban occurs somewhere in Leviticus or Deuteronomy, but it was imposed long afterward by the Pharisees of the first century B.C. as a cautious amplification of "Thou shalt not seethe a kid in its mother's milk."

Even smart international hotels, unwilling to offend orthodox guests, obey the religious authorities. Visiting bishops and ministers must, therefore, decide whether to order boiled beef and vegetables, followed by compote of fruit, or a cheese omelet, followed by compote of fruit and custard. Either the beef is off, or the custard is off. This "meat or dairy" alternative helps the economy of a country so short of the former, and the Book of Numbers contains a moral anecdote about the Israelite who lusted after flesh food in the Wilderness and died of a surfeit when the Lord in His anger sent them plentiful flocks of quail.

But if a certain foreign attache who told me these dietary rules lower national vitality was right, I dare not think what the result of their removal would be. A native-born Israeli is already the toughest and most vital human being I have come across anywhere.

ISRAEL AND GERMANY

DAVID BEN-GURION

No debate in the Knesset under Ben-Gurion's leadership aroused more heated argument and deeper passions than the question of Israel's trade relations with Germany, particularly the sale of munitions. On the following pages the former Prime Minister discloses his reasons for resuming normal relations with West Germany.

If you want the overall reason in a single sentence: it was the final injunction of the inarticulate six million, the victims of Nazism, whose very murder was a ringing cry for Israel to rise, to be strong and prosperous, to safeguard her peace and security, and so prevent such a disaster from ever again overwhelming the Jewish people. This was my key criterion when I faced the problem of Israel's relations with Germany.

It was a massive problem. Here was a country which had destroyed six million Jews in our generation, and if it had won the war, there is no doubt that it would have gained world domination and destroyed the entire Jewish people. Jewish history, which is replete with acts of slaughter against Jews, knows no parallel to the crimes of Nazi Germany. Deeds like hers can never be forgotten nor forgiven—certainly not by our generation, whose brothers and sisters, parents and children were murdered at Auschwitz, Treblinka, Chelmno and Belsen, Sobibor and Maidanek and

David Ben-Gurion. "Israel and Germany," *Ben-Gurion Looks Back.* Ed. by Moshe Pearlman. New York: Simon & Schuster, 1965.

many other places of dread. And I was proposing neither forgiveness nor wiping the slate clean when I presented the demand for reparations from West Germany at the Knesset session in January, 1952. (Incidentally, Eastern Germany has to this day refused any demand for the restoration of the spoils of those who were murdered by the Nazis in their region.) But I knew that the debate would be tempestuous and charged with emotion, and that this would be the mood both of the demagogues and also of the sincere opponents of contact with Germany. The demagogues did indeed seek to exploit the blood of the martyrs and rouse popular emotion against us—as if my feelings about the Nazi slaughter were less passionate than theirs—and they even tried to obstruct the Knesset during the debate. The sincere opponents thought quite simply that it was wrong to have anything to do with Germany and that even reparations from them were too loathsome to touch. I am glad that the majority of the Knesset members, and I think even the majority of the Jewish people both in Israel and abroad, did not take this attitude. They were in favor of negotiations with Adenauer's Germany, which had recognized the moral responsibility of the entire German people for the crimes of the Nazis and accepted the duty of compensating the surviving sufferers.

Many people find it difficult to free themselves from emotional moods of the past. They do not see the changes that take place in the world, the new relationships and the new needs. If we can do nothing about the disasters of the past, we can at least take steps to keep the future free of such happenings. And this we can do by examining the realities, not with the eyes of yesterday but with an insight into the patterns of change.

The discussion on reparations centered largely round the question of whether or not the Germany of today is the same Nazi Germany and whether there was any difference between Adenauer and Hitler. Some of my extreme opponents even held that you could go back to Imperial Germany and find no change in all the systems that followed; the German people had been and would always remain a Nazi people.

The debate was renewed when our Defense Ministry conducted negotiations with the German Defense Ministry. Actually my opponents did not now oppose negotiations, but they argued that these should not be conducted by a "high ranking personality," implying that it was permissible for them to be handled by lower level representatives. This is the kind of absurdity which can result if emotions are allowed to becloud the analysis of a problem.

There was a third great flare-up when the German paper, *Der Spiegel,* in July, 1959, reported the sale of arms from Israel to the West German Ministry of Defense. As a matter of fact, in December, 1958, I brought to the Cabinet the proposal that we sell Germany a quantity of small arms which we manufactured in Israel, and I got Cabinet approval. The contract was signed some three months later.

The idea of Israel's supplying arms to Germany was bound to provoke a good deal of interest in the world, for here was a country which had been known for generations as the military State par excellence, now buying arms from the very State whose blood brothers she had killed. On the face of it, it would seem a shameful and unpopular thing to do. But not on deeper analysis. And again I am glad to say that most of the newspapers in the world, both Jewish and non-Jewish, joined with the majority in the Knesset in recognizing the soundness and political maturity of the Government's action. After thinking through a problem and determining policy in accordance with what I believed to be the basic interests of Israel, it was always my rule, as Prime Minister, to try and put it into effect no matter how unpopular it might seem at first glance. This is one of the functions of leadership. No leader can advance the interests of his country if he is concerned only with courting popularity. I think that is one of the major weaknesses of the Arab leadership.

But you asked for my reasoning, and I have given you so

far mostly the immediate reactions to my German policy. I said a moment ago that deeper analysis of this policy would lead to a recognition of its soundness. Let me offer my analysis.

I have spoken of our six million victims of Nazism whom no mortal power can bring back, and of our need, as an independent people in our own land, to be able to stand up to our foes with our own strength so that the holocaust can never recur. A spurning of idle lament and a call to constructive deeds are implicit in this course of action. This, in fact, has been the approach of three generations of Israeli pioneers—the people who laid the foundations of statehood. This was the lesson they had learned from Jewish history in exile—the almost continuous chain of disaster, with the butcheries by the Crusaders, the expulsions from England and later from Spain and Portugal, the atrocities of the Russian Csars, of Petlura, of Hitler. The Zionist pioneers spent no time in weeping. Instead they resolved to devote all their energies to the revival of their homeland, to build Jewish villages, to accumulate Jewish strength, to arm, to intensify immigration, and eventually, to establish a State and become a sovereign people, an equal member in the family of nations.

Having achieved this, we had to safeguard our security. This is still threatened by our neighbors who maintain a state of war against us and seek to isolate us politically and economically. Moreover, their military strength is expanding constantly and they have ready sources of armaments, mostly from the Soviet bloc but also from the West. What must our answer be? Clearly both to maintain a military force skilled and well-equipped to serve as a deterrent, and to develop friendly relations with as many States as possible in Europe and America, Africa and Asia. This is important politically, since such friendship can eventually bring about a weakening of the Arab wall of hatred and pave the way to regional peace, and also militarily, since it guarantees sources of supply of needed armaments.

In developing relations with other countries, Germany included—I put my mind to the problem of Germany soon after the establishment of the State—I had to examine the realities of the world in which we lived and try to foresee the trends of international groupings. This was a very different world from the world of August, 1897, when Theodore Herzl wrote in his diary at the first Zionist Congress in Basle: "Today I have founded the Jewish State." Had the State been set up then, a Jewish Army would not have been an urgent need. For, at that time, the Jewish people had not suffered the loss of more than one-third of their numbers, all the gates were open, and European Jewry could have streamed into Israel. This Jewish State would have been regarded with favor by the whole of Europe, which then dominated the world, and there would have been not a single hostile neighbor on its borders, for in those days there were no Arab States in existence; the Middle East, including Egypt, was part of the Ottoman Empire. Israel, however, came into being not at the end of the nineteenth century but in 1948, and the Jewish people, the Middle East, and the rest of the world had now undergone fundamental changes.

Britain, France, Germany, powers of the first magnitude in the nineteenth and early part of the twentieth centuries, had now declined. At the head of the world stood two mighty nations, the United States and Soviet Russia. And soon, despite their own strength, each sought alliance with other countries to extend the defensive fringe beyond their own borders and improve their strategic positions. The United States initiated NATO and Russia formed the Warsaw Pact. Thus, almost all countries in the world today are linked to others by military and political pacts and alliances or by bonds of religion, language, tradition, or geography. Israel is almost the only country in the world which lives alone, having membership in no military or political alliance—though she is by no means morally neutral—sharing her religion and language and customs with no other State, and being cut off, through hostility, from her geographic neighbors. Her task of developing international relationships is, therefore, that much harder, though it must be said that because of it the friendships that are established are also more solidly based.

I think you can begin to see the reasoning process which led to our German policy. Because of the international groupings of which I have spoken, the aims of foreign policy must be to develop friendship not only with a particular country but if possible also with the group of which it is a part, promoting ties with the friends of friends. Now I do not hold, as do some of my opponents, that Germany today is the Germany of the Kaiser or of Hitler. I believe she will never again command her former influence; her days of hegemony in Europe have gone. But her international position grows in importance. She is a member of NATO and holds an important position in that alliance. Her relationship with the United States grows more friendly. Moreover—and this is of great moment for Israel—there is an increasing drive for unity among the nations of western Europe, and France, Israel's great friend, has started drawing closer to Germany. Just think of that for a moment. France, after suffering grievously on three outstanding occasions from assaults by Imperial and Hitlerite Germany—in the 1870's and in the two world wars—took the initiative to promote a special relationship between the two countries. General de Gaulle, that great French statesman, went to meet Dr. Adenauer in Bonn, addressed the German people in their own language, urged the importance of a rapprochement between the two historic rivals, and concluded an alliance of friendship. Does anyone doubt de Gaulle's patriotism? Does anyone conceive that he was acting out of weakness?

I do not think the alliance was concluded because the

French love the Germans or because the Germans love the French. I am sure that France, particularly the France of de Gaulle, has not forgotten what Imperial and Nazi Germany did to her. Yet, they started to draw closer to each other. This was prompted not by mutual love but by mutual need. Mutual interest—that is the basis of political friendship. And so there is an attempt at closer cooperation between the two countries, particularly on economic and military affairs. I do not know how long it will last, but at least the trend is there, even under Erhard.

Now if it is imperative that we maintain our warm relations with France—and I imagine everyone in Israel would agree that it is—then it would seem to be equally imperative that we develop friendly relations with France's friends including Germany. In determining foreign policy when I was Prime Minister, my obvious criterion, as is that of any leader of a State, was the degree to which a particular course would advance the interests of Israel. On this criterion, I initiated a policy of friendship to Germany.

Moreover, it is vital to Israel's interests that her Defense Forces should be strong. I have already told you that I do not think the security of a country rests only upon its military strength; in our case, land settlement, immigration, and education are also of great importance. But it is certainly true that we can have no security without an army, and an army's power is dependent on two basic elements—the spirit and skill of its fighting men and the weapons at their disposal. In the modern world, there are some types of armament which only a few countries can and do produce. Of these few, not all are prepared to sell them to us, even for payment in full. The Soviet bloc, which sends vast quantities of modern arms to the Arab countries, knowing well the purpose for which they are intended, refuses to supply Israel. This may also be the policy even of a country most friendly to Israel, the United States, for example. The United States is one of the principal manufacturers of arms in the world and a country with close bonds of friendship with Israel. Yet, for various reasons, up to only a comparatively short time ago, she refused to send us arms, even against payment. Only recently has she changed her policy and sanctioned our purchase of anti-aircraft missiles.

There has been a similar change in British policy. For a long time, Britain, both in the days of Bevin and later under Eden, was unsympathetic to Israel. Though she had signed the Tri-partite Declaration in 1950—the other two were France and the United States—undertaking to preserve the balance of forces between Israel and the Arab States, she refused to sell arms to Israel though she supplied them free of charge to Jordan and Iran and sold them to Egypt. However, the British Foreign Office became disenchanted with the Arabs in the Middle East after the revolution in Iraq in July, 1958, recognized that they were a broken reed and that Nasser was a grave danger both to the free world and to the liberties of the other Arab countries. Her relations with Israel improved after that, and she began to appreciate Israel's democratic regime, her achievements, and her growing importance in the international arena. This improvement in our relations expressed itself, among other things, in her readiness to supply our Defense Forces with tanks and submarines.

After the Czech arms deal with Egypt in the middle Fifties, Canada too was prepared—though after much hesitation—to sell us jet planes, so vital to us then. But by the time we received the Canadian answer, we were already receiving the much needed aircraft from France, Israel's loyal ally in Europe, first under the government of Edgar Faure and especially during the premiership of Guy Mollet. It was not worth while using different models, which would have necessitated different spare parts and maintenance methods, and so we turned down the Canadian planes. Since then, France has been Israel's major source of supply of those types of weapons which Israel does not herself produce. Britain and America, as I have said, are now also sources.

A factor to be remembered when considering the problem of arms, is that we must always think of the future. Equipping an army is not a one-time job. It is a continuous process. Military equipment becomes obsolete, today more quickly than ever before, and today more particularly with the more important weapons, the ones that can be decisive. And each new model is more and more complicated than the last. If our army is to be a true deterrent, the prime need for our defense and our survival, we must ensure that it is equipped and re-equipped every few years. For the enemies threatening our very existence can always be certain of receiving the finest and most modern equipment all the time. If Germany can be a source for the strengthening of Israel, then surely we must do what we can to keep that source open.

I do not suppose there is anyone in Israel who would not welcome closer friendship with the Soviet Union, Czechoslovakia, Hungary, and Rumania. But this does not depend on Israel. And I do not see it as a possibility in the near future. At the moment, there is not the slightest prospect of our being able to arm our forces with Soviet equipment like the armies of Egypt, Syria, Iran, and the Yemen. Israel would, therefore, be in mortal danger if she did not make an effort in good time to promote cordial relations with all the countries able and willing to strengthen her security.

This does not mean that our attitude to Germany is blindly uncritical. We have been most outspoken over the German Government's relative inactivity over the German scientists who are in Cairo helping Nasser to destroy Israel. And, of course, we must be alive to the dangers of German submission to Arab blackmail in the economic and political field. I am quite aware of the fact that there are still Nazis and anti-Semites in West Germany—just as there are in East Germany. (Nor can I say that we have no enemies in other countries—even in the United States and France.) But only those who live completely in the past and fail to see the changes that have taken place in the world can believe that Hitler's Germany may be resurrected. This is not only because the German regime has changed, but mainly because the geopolitical configuration of Europe and the world has changed. Germany, like Britain, can no longer lead the world and think that she can do exactly as she pleases. Not even the two giant powers, who head the rival blocs, can do as they please. Each needs and strives to secure the support of other peoples in the new world that came into being after the last war, and each is dependent to a great extent on world public opinion. Indeed, as I have said, the desire to gain sympathetic world opinion is a basic feature of the cold war.

Germany, then, to my mind, will never again be the kind of world power she was at the beginning of this century. But she is definitely a rising power. And it is clear that the great majority of the German people prefer to remain in the democratic camp despite—or because of—Soviet influence in the eastern part of the country and her desire for all Germany to be a Soviet satellite. To us, it cannot be unimportant whether West Germany is for or against Israel. Germany could well be a force hostile to Israel, since this is possible even without Nazis; there are no Nazis in India, yet the Indian Government shows no particular friendship for Israel. A hostile Germany might endanger the friendship with Israel of other peoples of western Europe and could also have an undesirable influence on the United States. It is, therefore, doubly important for Israel to promote closer relations with Germany.

You met Adenauer when you were Prime Minister. What did you think of him?

Yes, I met him in New York in 1960, but my estimate of him is based not only on my impressions of that meeting. I had followed his policies and achievements, and I had also had exchanges of correspondence with him. From all this I felt and feel that he will be remembered in German and in European history as one of the great statesmen of our time. To him must go the principle credit for the economic, political, and moral revival of his country after the disaster and disgrace of the Nazi regime.

ISRAEL ON THE EVE OF EICHMANN'S TRIAL

FLORA LEWIS

Adolf Eichmann, a principal figure in the Nazi extermination program of the Jewish people, which they euphemistically called "the final solution," eluded capture for fifteen years after the War. He was finally tracked down by Israeli agents in Argentina, where he had been living as Ricardo Klement, the second husband of the widow Frau Eichmann. He was surreptitiously spirited to Israel, where he was publicly tried, convicted, and hanged.

There are some people in Israel who say that, when the painful story has been retold and the verdict solemnly pronounced, Adolf Eichmann should be sent out to wander through the Jewish state—to gaze upon the rich profusion of the corn fields that hide yesterday's scrawny desert, to file through the grids of new suburban streets that were yesterday's fly-specked indolent village squares, to peer into the confident faces of a brawny lusty youth who spring from yesterday's helpless victims.

Whatever happens to Eichmann—the man, whose task was the "final solution of the Jewish problem" (mass murder)—his destiny is one he could never have envisaged despite the pains he took with everything. The extermination camps, with their bookkeeping on the value of gold teeth and human hair saved from incineration as against the cost of fuel, were meticulously organized to destroy all the people who were Jews. They served a large part of their appalling purpose.

Flora Lewis. "Israel on the Eve of Eichmann's Trial," *New York Times Magazine* (April 9, 1961).

But the culminating drama of this history is about to take place instead in a sedate courtroom. Here in Jerusalem, holy city and capital of a young and virile Jewish state, the man Adolf Eichmann will be solemnly judged by those he once condemned in their entirety. It is an extraordinary event. No ordinary thoughts of revenge or retribution enter into this symbol of the patient triumph of humanity over the human capacity for evil. In the thriving land of their own making, the people he tried to erase from the earth will this week call him to account for his crimes. It is, in the most immediate way, the accounting of history.

And, yet, it is the fields and the suburbs and the husky young that preoccupy Israelis on the eve of the Eichmann trial, for despite the man who is to stand this week before the bar of justice, they are in the flush of vigorous creation.

People point to a bare hilltop and say the new Parliament building will be there. They wave toward a stretch of sand dunes and say the truck and bus assembly plant is going up there. They huddle about a deal table in a plain cafe to argue whether a new power plant can be completed before the town's population doubles.

People speak of the present and the future, and only when pressed, do they turn to the past. For Israel now is a self-assured, self-absorbed country, proud and expectant, too busy and too eager for growth to feed on the bitter herbs of tragedy.

Still, there is a rustle of uneasiness as the time approaches to listen once more to the story of the Nazis and the Jews. It is the same stir of discomfort—a taut silence broken only by muffled shifts to ease the cramp of tension—that filled a Tel Aviv theatre during showings of the Swedish film "Mein Kampf."

Most of the audience that crammed the theatre night after night were Jews of the Middle East and Africa. There were also many young people who had learned in school that their forebears were persecuted by Germans and had calmly placed the fact on a mental pile of history alongside their troubles from the Pharaohs, the Philistines and the Romans.

They went into the theatre chattering, as people go to see a movie about Custer's Last Stand or the hordes of Genghis Khan. But they came out quietly, for they had seen neither sets nor actors but a grisly family album.

An Israeli named Itzhak Austrian told his wife, who is from Poland via Bergen-Belsen, that he was going out to play cards for a couple of hours with the boys. Then he sneaked off to see the film. She had had frantic nightmares for years after she reached Palestine in 1947, and he does all he can to protect her from anything that will dig up buried memories. But he felt compelled to see for himself.

Many people in Israel fear the Eichmann trial will provoke a wave of nervous breakdowns among the survivors of the concentration camps, outbreaks of hysteria among those whose wounds have scarred in a decade and a half of dealing with everyday life. Many fear that the recital of tragedy will cause fresh tragedy—exposing tales of collaboration which will have to be completed in new scandals, because not every victim behaved well in a time of terror. They fear, too, that the gap will widen between an older generation which learned the meaning of suffering through experience and a self-reliant, impatient youth.

"Why didn't the Jews fight back?" the children of the heroes of the Ghetto Kibbutz, founded by survivors from Warsaw, ask their parents. "Why did they just wait to be slaughtered; why didn't they run away?"

The answers are not comprehensible to the Israeli young, full of the triumphs of Israeli arms in the two wars their state has fought. Many—the children who have no grandparents, no aunts or uncles or cousins, because so few families escaped the Nazis—ask: "Who won in the end? The Germans or the Jews?"

The question hurt, and opinion is divided as to whether

it is right to prompt them by reopening the subject. Some, like Zwi Shner of the Warsaw survivors' kibbutz, who runs an archive and a museum on the Nazi persecutions, are fiercely convinced that it is necessary for all Israelis, for Germans, and for the rest of the world to know and to remember what happened.

"It was sixteen years ago," Shner said in a cool voice. "Sixteen years is too soon to forget."

Others ask in voices weary of hate: "If they caught Eichmann in Argentina, why couldn't they just spend a bullet and leave him there? Do we really need to go through this trial?"

The division is not reflected in the newspapers which have already come to take the impending Eichmann trial as one of those existing facts of life that it is pointless to question, like the crisis in Laos or the truculence of Moscow. The only thing is to get on with the problem and to do what has been made necessary.

Nor is it a cause for debate in the Government or in the cafes. The trial is coming, people acknowledge; so be it. The attitudes of apprehension, regret, determination to honor the dead and warn the living conflict quietly. People accept each other's right to a different view and avoid discussion when they see they disagree. It is a tacit avowal that different reasons brought them to Israel, but that their various pasts cannot splinter their common future.

Opinion is divided, too, on whether there should be good relations or bad relations or coldly correct relations with Germany now. But even among those who regret the need for trial, now that the man is here, many say it probably is good for Germans to be reminded of their cold-blooded crimes by Jews in a Jewish state, conducting due process of law through their own courts, exercising their own sovereign power.

And there is no doubt that the trial of Eichmann, a man and also a symbol of an evil time, will be a reminder. Most

Germans, preferring to break with their nation's past, have now no feeling of connection with Eichmann, no feeling of shared responsibility for him any more than most law abiding Americans felt responsible for Dillinger or Al Capone.

There is concern in the West German Government lest Eichmann's trial renew old hostilities in America and other Western countries whose friendship is one of the miracles of German revival. There is some impatience and irritation among the German public that the old ghosts are not laid in oblivion. And many people would rather not be interested, as though that would hasten the exercise.

But if there has been intense inattention among Germans to the prelude to the Eichmann trial, except perhaps to the narrow ways it might affect current politics through the involvement of post-war political names, it seems impossible that that unconcern will survive what is to pour forth from the courtroom.

In the pre-trial interrogations, Eichmann is said to have spoken freely. His own words, the sound of his voice, and the look on his face will be sent home by several scores of German correspondents. It is, after all, an integral piece of the Germans' immediate, and even personal, history. The trial cannot but compel German eyes to look both inward and toward Jerusalem, and hurtful questions will echo in Germany, too. There, no doubt, will lie the main if not the sole satisfaction of the Eichmann trial for Israelis.

If there is little craving for satisfaction, considering what might have been expected, it is because for all their daily grumbles, the Israelis find satisfaction in what they do and need not seek fulfillment in revenge for what was done to them.

The leading item on the news broadcasts the other day—a day when Egypt's Nasser made a threatening speech, when the Israeli Parliament moved toward dissolution and elections, when France arranged talks with Algerian rebels, when the Congo boiled—was that an Israeli soccer team had beaten Ethiopia, 3-2, and thus, was eligible to play Italy in the next round of the world championship matches. The sports fans were delighted with victory, and those not interested in sports were delighted to see that theirs was becoming a country of sports fans, released from overwhelming tensions and capable of hearty play.

And so, where the green Mediterranean foam breaks unhindered on miles of empty beach, a local official draws his index finger through the air to show where the deep-sea port will be.

The bulletin board of the new golf club at Caesarea promises a "valuable prize" to the winner of a competition to suggest Hebrew words for "golf," "fairway," "tee," "divot," "drive."

In Elath where the southern tip of Israel touches the Gulf of Aqaba, Shmulek Meltzer, who has a booming tourist-guide business, worries about the risk of marriage. Elath is a lonely town cut off from the rest of the country by the naked rock and the parched ochre-and-russet ground that is the wilderness of the Biblical wanderings in Sinai.

"Some fellows I knew down here got married," Shmulek said, "and then their wives said it was too rugged and made them move back north. I love this place and I can't take a chance of marrying a girl who'll get tired of it and nag at me not to stay."

In the north, on the hills of Galilee, a Texan started a course to train cowboys. Now a lad called Lolik spanks his guitar at The End of the World, Elath's low-ceilinged, candle-lit cabaret, and sings songs of the saddle and the campfire in a clear, gentle voice, drawling out the aspirate Hebrew sounds.

In Beersheba, an elegant, lively woman named Dita Natzor brushes aside the admiring introduction she is given as an early resident. "I used to be proud," she said, "but it is nothing now. It is no hardship to live in Beersheba. We have sidewalks and supermarkets." And her eyes glitter because, nonetheless, she is still awed and amused by such developments in the sleepy desert town she has chosen as home.

Along the waterfront at Tel Aviv, platoons of Army girls march along looking blowzy in their crumpled fatigues and heavy boots. One platoon is singing "Meadowland" with much more vim than harmony. And when young men drive by the girls whistle and wave in a twist of the traditional, soldierly way.

There is plenty to talk about in the cafes and farm cottages and the square sitting-dining rooms of the boxy, low apartments buildings, plunked in endless, neat rows around each town as though an orderly child had been given a bottomless bag of blocks and never tired of setting them out. The talk is of taxes and movies, crops and politics, love affairs and travel.

Security is a persistent problem, of course. "Everybody lives on the border here," people say with a shrug when they are asked if it makes them uneasy to know that if they walk a bit too far along the path ahead or swim a bit too far into the sea they will be in hostile territory. But there is no sign of worry in the shrug. Sooner or later there will be peace with the Arabs, they tell you comfortably. A Yemenite woman's eyes shine with pleased expectancy as she says, "It should be very soon. There is no good to anyone in the quarreling. I like the Arabs. We always lived together as very good friends."

The population is almost equally divided now between Jews of the Orient and of Europe, Jews from the lands of Islam and from Christian countries. They have not had an easy time living together, and when a son of one group weds a daughter of the other, it is called an intermarriage (they are now running at 20 per cent of all marriages, the authorities say).

If people talk about the past, it is usually in a tightly restricted and personal way, avoiding the enormity that is too much for an individual to bear.

A hotel manager mentions, in a manner that would seem casual except for a steely flash in his gray eyes, that the burn scars on his chest were made deliberately with Gestapo-issue cigarettes. But he would rather talk about his later experiences in the Jewish underground, and as for Eichmann, he says only: "There is no way to punish such a man. All you can do is remove him from the earth."

A shopkeeper remembers the grand piano and the heavily carved furniture in his family home at Dortmund, and his wife points out that it is more difficult to bring up children without grandparents. They do not go into the rest of their personal history.

A nurse explains the series of freak incidents that put her into the work-camp line instead of the gas-chamber line each time the roll was called at Auschwitz. Her eyes suddenly moisten and go red at the rims, and she skips the rest of the story, saying only: "I weighed fifty-eight pounds when I was liberated, but now I'm plump again. I don't need to be reminded of Eichmann. I need to go on with my life."

When Israelis do allow their inner eye to scan the breadth of horror, it is more to enhance an achievement that arose from such ashes than to see whence the phoenix mounted. The relevance of the Eichmann trial to most of them is precisely that he represents the past and sharpens the confident outline of the present. His pertinence is that he no longer matters very much, and other concerns can be allowed to dominate Israeli minds.

A New Zealander, who came to the Middle East with the Anzac armies in the war, fancied the place, and returned to stay, was upset at the bitter note of the concentration-camp museum.

To him, the point of Israel is for it to be a normal, healthy country, with brave and devoted people—and cranks and criminals and greedy people, perhaps—but, above all, a place where being Jewish is no more difficult than being Catholic in Ireland. He wondered whether it was proper here to display the wounds of hatred other people have inflicted and to try to explain to children who cannot fathom what anti-Semitism means.

Slowly, the hard way, Israel has been coming to be a calm country in the sixteen years since Adolf Eichmann lost by force of arms his job of liquidation and went into hiding. The Jews of Israel have been getting on with the business of making their life—adding a different-toned chapter to the long and painful history that the Nazis sought to close with a "final solution."

There is, of necessity, a sadness and an anger when they think about the past, and the past is there beyond erasure. But the book was not closed, and now a new page is being written.

David Ben-Gurion, the Israeli Premier, has a keen sense of history. It was the infusion of this sense that provided much of the morale required to build his state. Most of his people accept, though a great many of them do so with reluctance, that the necessary sense of history also requires an Israeli reckoning of the score.

For the Government officials directly involved, it has meant a frenetic spate of preparation. Ben-Gurion vetoed a proposal to use Jerusalem's convention hall, with some 2,500 seats, for the trial, and instead, it will be held in a newly completed Government building with seats for about 600—"enough for the serious participants, not enough for sightseers and the idly curious" as a Government spokesman explained.

Some 400 foreign correspondents are expected, along with lawyers and semi-official observers from a score of countries, and that means a fierce strain on Jerusalem's limited hotel space. Special communications facilities have to be arranged, multilingual operators and drivers hired. Censorship, on dispatches about the trial itself, is to be lifted. Around the pink stone building, workmen have put up a high wire fence to keep the curious at bay.

Altogether, Israelis agree, it is a difficult and an uncomfortable undertaking, this rendering of justice on a single man for the death and degradation of so many millions. When they discuss the trial, they are more likely to quibble about the details than about the larger meaning.

It is not, the Government officials state firmly, to be a show trial. Every curlicue and tangle of legal procedure—based in Israel on Anglo-Saxon common law—must be painstakingly followed to the end. And, yet, the purpose is so clearly one of demonstration rather than of judgment that absurdities keep cropping up. There is a hollow argument on whether all the judges are really unbiased and objective. There is sniffing about whether the defense will be permitted to be full and fair. These are the specifics of unreality.

It sounds as if the trial of Adolf Eichmann were to be conducted in a different world orbiting around a different sun from the one that shone through the incinerator smoke above Auschwitz and Maidanek and Treblinka and the many other names of hell on this earth.

And that is probably the case. The atmosphere and the place where Eichmann will be judged is a universe removed from the one he tried to create. That atmosphere, the mood of Israel today, is reflected in the way its people measure the time that constitutes current history.

"It was only sixteen years ago—too soon to forget," said a man who went back to his home town of Kassel and found that his grandparents' graves had been obliterated along with his living relatives.

"Thirteen years is a very long time. Everything has changed a lot," said a Tel Aviv bus driver, comparing the sprawling city with the patchy town of 1948 when Israel won independence.

"In three or four years there will be five new cities between Beersheba and Elath," said a pipefitter at the copper mines near King Solomon's smelters. "We won't be isolated then."

"In seven or eight years the economy will be sound, practically self-supporting," said the spokesman of the central bank.

It is predominantly a forward-looking mood.

ISRAEL: LAND OF UNLIMITED IMPOSSIBILITIES

BARBARA W. TUCHMAN

When you consider Israel's staggering problems, it is a wonder the tiny country exists at all. Thus, when an Israeli Rabbi insists that the usual solution to any given crisis is a miracle (not to mention the miracle that would take place if a solution was ever devised in the usual way), we are hard put to disagree!

No nation in the world has so many drastic problems squeezed into so small a space, under such urgent pressure of time and heavy burden of history, as Israel. In a country the size of Massachusetts, all included in one telephone book, it must maintain national existence while subject to the active hostility of four neighbors jointly pledged to annihilate it. Under their boycott it is cut off from trade, transportation, and communication across its entire land frontier. In this situation it must perform three vital functions at once: maintain a state of military defense at constant alert, forge a coherent nation out of a largely immigrant population, and develop an economy capable both of supporting defense and absorbing the continuing flow of newcomers who now outnumber the founders of the state by two to one. It speaks a language, Hebrew, distinct from any other both in grammatical structure and alphabet, which must be learned on arrival by virtually all immigrants. To

Barbara W. Tuchman. "Israel: Land of Unlimited Impossibilities," *The Saturday Evening Post* (January 14, 1967).

become self-sufficient in food, or by trade in food, it must restore fertility to the soil and reclaim the desert. Half of its land is non-arable except by irrigation, and its water supply is both inadequate and under threat of diversion by the Arabs. It must create industry where there was none and compete with more developed countries for foreign markets. It must operate with two official languages, Hebrew and Arabic, plus a general use of English; two sets of schools, religious and lay; and three forms of law, Ottoman, English, and rabbinical. While carrying the living memory of the mass murder of European Jewry who would have been its reservoir of population, and whose survivors and sons and daughters are among its citizens, it must, out of necessity, accept financial "restitution" and economic assistance from the nation of the murderers.

The drama of the struggle is in the atmosphere and in the facts of life. It is in the half-finished buildings of poured concrete going up on every hand, the most ubiquitous sight in Israel; in the intense faces of a class in an ulpan where adults from 20 countries learn Hebrew in five months; in the draft for military service, which takes every citizen of both sexes at 18; in the barbed wire dividing Jerusalem, and in the empty house in no-man's-land, still standing as it was left 18 years ago with shattered walls and red-tiled roof fallen in; in the sudden sound of shots on a still Sabbath morning from the northern shore of the Sea of Galilee; in the matter-of-fact underground shelter dug in the yard of a kibbutz kindergarten near the Syrian border, with two benches against earth walls and a concrete door always open; in the fantastic machinery and belching smokestacks of phosphate works in the Negev; in the weed-grown dirt streets and emergency shacks of a new village where a bearded Jew from Morocco stares out of dull eyes at a strange land, and a Hungarian Jew with more hope has hung out a sign, SALON BUDAPEST—HAIRDRESSING; in the compulsive talk of plant manager, government official, or school principal as they explain to a visitor what conditions were like five years ago and what they will be five years hence; in the energy of marching youth groups on a mass hike, singing and swinging as they walk, with a purposefulness almost too arrogant; in plant nurseries with millions of pine and cypress seedlings for reforestation of the barren hills; in two figures on the wharf at Haifa after a ship has come in—an immigrant father locked in the arms of a waiting son as if all the deaths and griefs of the lost six million were enclosed in their wordless long embrace.

The landscape, too, is dramatic, both in Israel and Jordan, which together make up the country of the Bible. Seeing it at firsthand, one realizes it was no accident that God was invented, and two religions originated here. In the desert with its endless horizon by day and brilliance of stars at night, the vastness of the world would make a man lonely without God. The grotesque pillars of basalt and eroded sandstone on the shores of the Dead Sea, the red mountains of Edom, the weird gulfs and crags and craters of the Negev, could not have failed to make him wonder what immortal hand or eye had shaped them. If he saw God in a burning bush, one recognizes the bush today in the blaze of yellow blossoms on the broom, as well as the origin of another story in the extraordinary brightness of the star hanging over Jerusalem (and over Bethlehem, five miles away in Jordan). To Abraham and his progeny, the supernatural would have seemed close at hand in the sudden ferocity of cloudbursts that can wipe out a village or in rainbows of startling vividness with all the colors and both ends visible. Even the sun does not set reasonably here, as it does in the Western Hemisphere, but drops all at once in what seems less than a minute from the time its lower rim first touches the Mediterranean horizon. Visions like miracles occur in the constant play of moving clouds across the sun, as when a hilltop village or ruined crusaders' castle will suddenly be picked out in a spotlight of sunshine and then, when a passing cloud blots out the light, as suddenly fade into the shadowed hills and vanish. A suffused pale light, sometimes luminous gray, sometimes almost white, constantly changing, shines always on Jerusalem, and when the sun's rays shoot skyward from behind a cloud, one sees instantly the origin of the halo.

The past lies around every corner. Herod's tomb is next door to one's hotel in Jerusalem. And at Megiddo, the site of Armageddon that dominates old pathways from Egypt to Mesopotamia, archaeologists have uncovered the strata of 20 cities, including Solomon's with its stalls for 4,000 horses and chariots. The past is seen from one's car on the way to Tiberias, where workmen cutting into the road bank have laid bare a row of Roman sarcophagi. It lies on the beach at Caesarea, where one's shoe crunches on a broken shard of ancient pottery. One is sitting on it when picnicking on a grass-covered tel, or mound, thought to be the site of Gath, where Goliath came from. One walks on it along the crusaders' ramparts of Acre, where Richard the Lion-Hearted fought Saladin, or on the hill of Jaffa overlooking the harbor besieged by Napoleon. It is present, if somewhat obscured by cheap souvenirs, at Nazareth.

Archaeology is a national occupation, hobby, and in a sense, the national conscience. The government maintains a department for the exploration and study, preservation and display of ancient sites and monuments. Students in summertime volunteer for "digs." Although private digging is forbidden, a national hero like General Moshe Dayan, who is not easily restrained, pursues it with the intensity he applied to the Sinai campaign, piecing together amphorae from fragments in his studio and dragging home two entire Roman columns to set up in his garden—not without stirring up the usual wrangling in the newspapers, another favorite Israeli sport. The most spectacular recent work, under the direction of another wartime hero, General (now Professor) Yigael Yadin, is the uncovering of Masada, high on the cliffs above the Dead Sea, where in 73 A.D., after the fall of Jerusalem,

960 Jewish zealots holding out against Roman siege with the energy of despair finally committed mass suicide rather than surrender. Not far away, in Dead Sea caves reached by rope and helicopter, Yadin's team found further reminders of ancient valor in the letters of Simon Bar Kochba, who in 132-35 A.D., raised the remnants of Palestinian Jewry and maintained for three years the last battle for independence against Roman rule.

To feel itself a nation, a people must have not only independence and territory but also a history. For Israelis, so long and so widely dispersed, the distant past is important and the recent past even more so. Both the mass disaster, or Holocaust as they call it, suffered under Hitler, and the War of Independence against the Arabs in 1948, pervade the national consciousness and have their memorials on every hand. For Arabs the memory of 1948 is full of gall, but for Israelis it is heroic and they leave its momentos in place with deliberate pride. Along the road up to Jerusalem, so bitterly fought for in 1948, the rusted relics of their home-made armored cars have been left where they fell under fire. A captured Syrian tank stands in the village of Degania and a Bren-gun carrier in the garden of the kibbutz Ayelet Hashachar. A ship named Af-Al-Pi-Chen ("In Spite of Everything"), one of those which ran the British blockade to bring in illegal immigrants, has been hauled up as a monument where it landed at the foot of Mt. Carmel, on the road a few miles south of Haifa.

Unforgotten and unforgettable, the memory of the Germans' extermination of the majority of Europe's Jews is no less a part of the nation's history. Six million trees to reforest the Judean hills have been planted as a "Forest of Martyrs" in the name of the six million dead, as well as an avenue of trees for each of the "Righteous Gentiles" who, at risk to themselves in Gestapo-controlled Europe, saved and hid Jewish neighbors. A central archive of material on the extermination has been established, and it supplied much of the evidence for the Eichmann trial. In itself the trial was a form of memorial, for its main object was perhaps less to bring a war criminal to justice than to solidify the historical record. The archive is housed in the dark new memorial to the dead called the Yad Vashem, unquestionably the most impressive building in Israel. Nowhere has architectural form more clearly and unmistakably expressed an idea and an emotion. It stands on a hill outside Jerusalem—a low, square, forbidding structure on a stark plaza, with walls of huge, rounded stones, each like a dead man, surmounted by a heavy lid of wood that seems to press down with the weight of centuries. The building is unadorned by lettering or decoration of any kind. Indoors a raised walk behind a railing surrounds a bare stone floor. Flat on its surface, so that one looks down on them, lie in metal letters the names of the concentration camps: Auschwitz, Buchenwald, Dachau, Bergen-Belsen, Theresienstadt, and the others. A memorial flame burns in one corner. There is nothing else, and nothing else is needed. The building is a coffin and a grave, a monument to death.

Groups of visitors, Israeli and foreign—Americans, Scandinavians, Italians, French—come daily to stand at the railing, shaken, or silently weeping, or just uneasy. Like the seated Lincoln brooding in his marble hall on the Potomac, the Yad Vashem leaves no one unmoved. Israel, as the state whose people were the immediate victims, is the nearest heir of the tragedy (apart from Germany, which is another matter). As such it keeps the memory alive, not merely to mourn but with a sense, perhaps, of some mission to history.

At Almagor, a hilltop settlement in northern Galilee where clashes with Syria involving machine guns, tanks, and aircraft took place during the past two summers, one looks down on a silver stream winding through a green delta to the lake. The stream is the River Jordan, where it enters the Sea of Galilee (otherwise Lake Tiberias). The land on its far bank, backed by a range of hills, is Syria, with snow-capped

Mt. Hermon looming hugely in the distance. On one of the hills is a cluster of the Arabs' characteristic flat-topped sandstone huts, many of them painted pale blue to ward off evil. Down on the delta, black cattle graze, white egrets stand on the sand flats of the river, Arab families and farmers go about their business. The air is filled with a spring breeze and the twittering of birds, the hillside with weeds and wild flowers blossoming as profusely as a garden. Lavender thistle mixes with blue gentian, daisies with wild mustard and wild pink geranium, and scarlet poppies are scattered everywhere. A solitary young soldier sits with binoculars on a pile of stones, intently scanning the hills opposite.

Almagor is a settlement founded by Nahal, a pioneer corps in which military training and land cultivation are combined in a system Israel has developed to defend and simultaneously settle the frontier. The young recruit points to a long, straight scar on the side of the hill opposite and says it is the track of the Arabs' attempted diversion of the headwaters of the Jordan. Involving 75 miles of open ditch, the scheme could hardly be carried out secretly and is not an operation that Israel could idly watch. After the Syrians started shooting in August, 1965, the Israelis' answering fire, according to their communique, damaged "tractors at work in Syria on the diversion of the Jordon headwaters," after which the work "appeared to cease for the time being." When I was there in March before last summer's battle, the hillside scar, from what anyone could tell through binoculars, was quiescent.

Down on the lake, which is wholly Israeli territory, two fishing boats were moving out from the Syrian shore. The soldier remarked without heat that last year Syrian guns in the hills fired on an Israeli fishing boat and a cruising police patrol boat. Handing me the binoculars, he pointed to two black dots far out in the center of the lake. Slowly moving into vision, they took shape as Israeli police boats. The Syrians kept on fishing, and the patrols approaching. Gripping the binoculars, I waited, feeling as if the air had suddenly gone still. The police were within hailing distance when, unhurriedly, the Syrians rowed back to shore, beached their boats, and wandered off. Equally without fuss the patrol boats turned back the way they had come. Almagor remained quiet for that day.

The hillside scar, mentioned on return to Jerusalem, aroused no excitement. "It could be a road," they said. Israel so desperately needs peace—to divert taxes from the crushing defense budget to other vital needs, to rejoin the continent of which it is a part, to live with neighbors on reasonably neighborly terms, above all, to breathe normally—that it has usually leaned over backwards to avoid cause for quarrel. It tries to remain suave and, for as long as possible, unprovoked, in the effort to leave room for whatever tiny chance of negotiation might appear. Israel too has its hotheads of irredentism, the "adventurists" who clamor to "take the west bank," but this is largely lip service to old slogans. They know, or if not the country's leaders know, that to swallow western Jordan with nearly a million Arab inhabitants (or equally the Gaza Strip), thus increasing Israel's existing Arab minority of 12 percent who already outbreed the Jews, would be to court disaster. What Israel needs is not more land populated by Arabs but more people to populate its own empty Negev, a problem which in turn depends on water to make the desert habitable.

Even the wound of the Old City's loss is not so fresh anymore. For Jews its essence was the Wailing Wall for bewailing lost Zion, but since restoration of the state, who needs to wail? From long association, many still yearn for the Wall, but the native-born generation are not wailers. On their own land the Jews have successfully become what they were never allowed to be in the ghetto—farmers and soldiers. The transformation has literally changed the Jewish face. Complexion and lighter hair-color can no doubt be explained by sun and climate; blue eyes one must leave to the geneticists; but the fundamental change is one of expression. The new face has an outdoor look and, more noteworthy, it is cheerful. This is not of course true of the immigrant settlements, where the look among the adults is compounded of bewilderment, strangeness, difficulties, and resentments, nor of Tel Aviv, which has been unkindly (if not inaccurately) described as a mixture, on a smaller scale, of New York and West Berlin. The Tel Aviv look, compounded of traffic, shops, business deals, and culture, with a sprinkling of beatniks, is no different from the urban the world over.

The new face is elsewhere, notably in the army. At the officers' training school outside Tel Aviv, it was visible in students, instructors, and in the commandant, Colonel Meier Paeel, a tall, vigorous, smiling man. Colonel Paeel had smile crinkles at the corners of his eyes, a characteristic I noticed among many of the other officers, although someone else might say it came from squinting at the sun.

The school had pleasant tree-lined quarters inherited from the British Army, which was always accustomed to do itself well. The tradition continues in one respect, for the secretaries, all girl soldiers in khaki, were so invariably pretty, without makeup, that it was hard to believe they had been chosen at random. Because of its essential role in the creation of the state, the army's prestige is high, and it attracts the best. It has a noticeably breezy air. The open shirt collar—spotless and correctly starched—prevails. Saluting is casual, but there is an underlying seriousness and sense of tension. At the general-staff school, where virtually all the students wore the two campaign ribbons of 1948 and 1956, there was once again the outdoor face, and a commandant, Colonel Mordecai Goor, no less handsome and confident. "You are making a new breed," I said to one officer. He looked around thoughtfully at his colleagues and, searching for the right English words, replied deliberately, "Yes. Jewish sorrow has gone out of their eyes."

Reclamation of the land, after centuries of being strangers and rootless in the lands of others, has helped to achieve that result as much as anything. The Jews are at home; not a home taken over ready-made, but one they had to clear, clean, repair, and reconstruct by their own labor. Palestine, under Arabs and Turks during the thousand years before 1900, reverted to the nomad and, for lack of cultivation, was left to the desolation predicted by Isaiah: a "habitation of dragons and a court for owls." English explorers in the 19th century found it a stony goat pasture with "not a mile of made road in the land from Dan to Beersheba." To be made livable again, reported the Palestine Exploration Fund in 1880, the land required roads for wheeled transport, irrigation and swamp drainage, restoration of aqueducts and cisterns, sanitation, seeding of grass, and reforestation to check soil erosion. This was the task that faced, and all but overwhelmed, the early Jewish colonists. Internal dissension and self-made problems, as prevalent then as today, did not help. While they starved, they engaged in furious dispute over whether to keep the commandment of a sabbatical year, during which no work on fields or among livestock could be done.

The issue survives. At Kfar Yuval, a little colony in northern Galilee settled by an Orthodox group of Indian Jews, a schoolteacher apologized for the weed-grown yard that could not be cultivated because it was sabbatical year for the village. When I asked, "What do they eat?" my guide shrugged and said, "They pray and eat less." The fossilized rules of Orthodoxy hamper progress and convenience in the nation out of all proportion to the number who take them seriously. Because the Orthodox party holds the political balance of power, it has an official grip on the country, and Orthodoxy strikes a visitor as the most stultifying of Israel's self-made problems.

Yet, the Jews have made the land bloom—with terraced hills and delicate orchards, hedges of rosemary, and the thick lush green of orange groves. Everywhere around the groves in springtime, the pungent, sweet fragrance of orange blossom hangs in the air like smoke. Yellow mimosa and feathery, pine-like tamarisks grow along the roadside, punctuated by great cascades of purple bougainvillaea. Away from the urban strips and gas stations and industrial plants and somewhat shoddy emergency settlements, Israel has an extraordinary beauty. Cypresses, like dark green candles, point upward against the blue sky, and windblown olive trees shimmer as if their leaves were tipped with silver. When the wind blows, the palms bend like reeds over Lake Tiberias, and from western Galilee, one can see, far in the distance between the hills, the whitecaps of the Mediterranean glint in the sun.

It is no wonder the Jews have grown a new face. Perhaps what accounts for it most of all is that Israel is theirs; here, they are not a minority; they are on top. Which is not to say they will live happily ever after, or even now, for they are the most contentious people alive, and Orthodoxy is not their only self-made problem. Their quarrels are legion; they abuse each other incessantly and without compunction and settle differences of opinion within any group by splitting instead of submitting to majority rule. The Haifa Technion, Israel's M.I.T., was recently plunged in battle over the teaching of architecture. The issue, roughly one between scientific and humanistic schools of thought, exists in other countries as well, but the solution in Israel was radical. By dictate of the Technion's president, the faculty of architecture was split into two faculties—a decision which enraged the students, since they would have to choose between one or the other, and many wanted elements of both. Carried over to political life, the habit causes factionalism which Israelis explain as the natural consequence of long centuries without political power or responsibility. They consider that the experience of self-government is gradually providing an enforced cure.

Israel is not an affluent society; it is hard-working with

the six-day week still in force. Until last March, Israel had no television. This circumstance grew from the strong puritan strain of the early settlers, who were founders of Histadrut, the labor federation, and of the kibbutzim. Although the kibbutz system of communal ownership is neither predominant nor spreading, the influence of its people is out of proportion to their numbers because they came early, were self-motivated and, to survive at all, had to have vigor and grit. Kibbutz members in government took the view, violently disputed, that TV would distract from work, disrupt family life, and intensify economic and class differences between settled residents and the newcomers who could not afford to buy television sets. Besides, it would cost money, and the government had none to spare on a luxury. The awkward result is that anyone who buys a TV set, and that includes a large number of Arab citizens, tunes in Cairo or Beirut. Since last March, educational television is being tried.

Because Israel is a small country, the individual is able to feel that what he does counts. No more powerful incentive exists. It will make a man work even at a job he dislikes. One government official, who detested going abroad to beg for funds for an essential operation, told me he continued to go because he felt "on the front line of defense." Seeking something of this feeling, students from abroad, particularly Scandinavian refugees from too much welfare, come every summer to work in the kibbutzim.

With all its problems, Israel has one commanding advantage—a sense of purpose: to survive. It has come back. It has confounded persecution and outlived exile to become the only nation in the world that is governing itself in the same territory, under the same name, and with the same religion and same language as it did 3,000 years ago. It is conscious of fulfilling destiny. It knows it must not go under now, that it must endure. Israelis may not have affluence or television or enough water or the quiet life, but they have what affluence tends to smother—a motive. Dedication is not necessarily total, and according to some who see materialism displacing the idealism of the early days, it is already slipping. Israelis are not all true, honest, loyal, industrious—a nation of Boy Scouts. Many (an estimated total of 80,000–90,000 so far) leave for more pay (Israeli salaries are low and taxes high), more comfort, wider opportunities and contacts, a life of less pressure, or for a variety of reasons which add up to one—to escape geography. But on the whole and for the present, the pacesetters of the nation have what Americans had at Plymouth Rock, a knowledge of why they are there and where they are going. Even the visitor begins to feel that there may be a design to history after all, a purpose in the survival of this people who, ever since Abraham came out of Ur to mark the turn to Monotheism, have fertilized civilization with ideas—from Moses and Jesus to Marx, Freud, and Einstein. Perhaps survival is their fate.

Paradoxically, Arab hostility has been useful in forcing Israel to face westward, to find her contacts and competition with the West, including a trade agreement with the European Common Market. While this exacerbates the problem of acclimating her growing proportion of Oriental Jews from Iraq, Iran, and North Africa, it also drives her to greater enterprise, to "think deeper," as the manager of the Timna Copper Mines said. "Of course," he added a little wistfully, "if we had the whole of the Middle East to trade with we would have an easier life." As it is, necessity has required the development of such enterprises as his own, the former mines of King Solomon, unexploited under the Turks or the British Mandate and now restored to production by Solomon's descendants.

Timna is one of those projects, like almost everything in Israel, undertaken against the soundest advice of practical persons who declared it "impossible." Originally, the resettlement of Palestine was impossible, the draining of malarial swamps impossible, the building on sand dunes (where Tel

Aviv now has a population of over 600,000) impossible; the goal of statehood, partition, self-defense, the Law of Return, absorption of a million immigrants, then of two million immigrants—all impossible. The country has been created out of impossibilities, embraced sometimes from idealism, more often because there was no other choice.

Since no one would invest in a dead copper mine, Timna was subsidized and its shares taken up by the government; during the first three years of effort to begin operations, the project drew sarcastic press comment about "putting gold in the ground to get out copper." Now, with production booming, and a convenient world shortage caused by strikes in Chile and by Rhodesia's troubles, it is exporting 10,000 tons of copper cement a year, at explosively profitable prices, to Spain, Japan, and Hungary, while the public offers to buy the government's shares. No one expects this happy condition to last forever, but future, even present limitations frequently fail in Israel to have a limiting effect. If Israelis looked ahead at the stone wall or ditch looming up, they would stop dead from sheer fright; instead, they go on out of optimism or necessity and trust that God, or their own inventiveness, or some unforeseen development, will provide.

Out of such necessities, the country finds its resources. To compete with Italy in the export of oranges, for example, an Israeli fruit grower joined with a village farm-machinery factory to invent an ingenious motorized orange-picking machine that consists of two raised platforms on a wheeled hoist and permits faster, cheaper harvesting. The Arid Zone Research Center in Beersheba has shown that the warm, sheltered climate of the Wadi Araba in the southern Negev can, with careful utilization of rain runoff from the hills, produce four crops a year. This makes possible the export to Europe of luxury out-of-season vegetables and fruits, such as the strawberries that are flown to European ski resorts.

A rather more major enterprise is Israel's "dry Suez," the pipeline which brings Iranian oil from Eilat on the Red Sea to Haifa and Tel Aviv on the Mediterranean. Built in answer to Nasser's exclusion of Israel from the Suez Canal, one 8 inch and one 16 inch line, with a capacity of 4.5 million tons a year, already exist. They were chiefly financed by Baron Edmond de Rothschild on condition of a guaranteed return; he has since made two and a half times his original investment. The ditch for a third line can be seen cutting its way through the Negev toward a terminus on the Mediterranean at the new deep-sea port of Ashdod, opened in 1965. Chiefly for the use of foreign oil companies as a supplement to the tanker route through the Suez Canal, the new Israeli pipeline may, depending on eventual size of the pipe and cost of service, one day undercut Suez rates.

The Negev itself, known in the Bible as the "Wilderness of Zin," is the prime "impossible." Although it accounts for more than 55 percent of Israel's land area, its capacity to absorb any increase of population was said by the Peel Commission, the most authoritative of the many which investigated Palestine's troubles during the Mandate, to be nil. Nevertheless, from 1948 through 1964, the number of people supported by the area has risen from 21,000 to 258,000, including the cities of Beersheba and Ashkelon, which are not strictly in the desert but on its northern edge. The rest are scattered among some 130 settlements, including Sde Boker, a kibbutz established in the middle of the desert as a magnet and an example, where Ben-Gurion has chosen to live. This population is greater than the estimated 30,000 to 60,000 which the Negev supported at its height in Roman and Byzantine times, when the system of guiding rainwater through man-made channels to cisterns was brought to engineering perfection. The Israelis consider themselves capable of no less, up to the limit of the rains from heaven. But modern man uses more water than the ancients; moreover, to bring more people to the Negev, necessitates the finding of new sources by any means creative intelligence can devise. Investigators are testing methods of inducing artificial rainfall, of using unpotable brackish water for irrigating salt-resistant crops, of enforcing water saving by metering water, of reducing evaporation in reservoirs by coating the surface with a fatty substance. But the ultimate answer for populating the Negev must be desalinization of seawater. A joint Israeli-American study is now under way for a future plant which, one is confidently told, will be ready by 1971. Powered by a nuclear reactor, it is expected to produce more than 30 billion gallons a year at reasonable cost. On the other hand, a recent report of the Weizmann Institute states that while it is possible by desalinization to provide fresh water in limited amounts for users "not sensitive" to the cost, "it is still an open question whether methods suitable for large-scale and *cheap* production of fresh water will ever be found."

Beersheba, once a dusty market town with an Arab population of 3,000 (who decamped in the war of 1948), began with a Jewish population of zero. Two hundred families came in 1949. As a result of the opening of the Negev by road and railroad, the development of chemical industries in the Dead Sea area, and a mass influx of immigrants, Beersheba has so exploded that a harried municipal councilor hastily scribbled new figures on a fact sheet before handing it to me. The population is, or was last spring, 72,000, of whom 85 percent are immigrants, half Orientals and half from Europe and South America. The city still serves as a center for some 16,000 Bedouin citizens of Israel, who live in the desert in their long black goat-hair tents. Everyone rushes, everyone is harried (except the Bedouin and the inevitable "tourist" camel who waits inappropriately in front of a filling station). Trash flies about in the wind; streets are half-paved; rubble and debris of building construction lie around; tattered posters advertise the city's seven movie houses; and the shell of an empty, circular, concrete building with a crenelated top, looking something like a child's cardboard crown, excites one's curiosity. "It's the synagogue," I am told with an impatient shrug. "The funds ran out. There are other things more important."

Schools, for instance. Beersheba has 32 elementary schools, each with a kindergarten, two high schools, and three trade schools, as well as a training school for teachers and one for nurses, an ulpan for immigrant adults, a yeshiva, and a music school. In order to keep students in the area, it has even last year started a university. Not degree-granting yet, it operates without a campus or faculty of its own, but with visiting professors lent by other institutions. Courses in the humanities and social sciences, one in biology, and a postgraduate course in engineering are offered to 260 students—a figure which, according to the regular Israeli refrain, "will be doubled next year." Nevertheless, a problem remains: There are not enough high schools in the Negev to fill up a university.

Beersheba is a microcosm—or it might be called a hothouse—of the nation's immigration problem, which cannot be envisaged without a few figures. In three and a half years from May, 1948 to the end of 1951, while the new state was struggling to its feet under a new government, 685,000 persons entered Israel, or slightly more than the population existing at the time the state was proclaimed. In 1950, the Knesset (parliament) enacted the Law of Return, confirming the right of every Jew to enter the country unless he has been guilty of offenses against the Jewish people or is a danger to public health or security. (The law was soon to raise interesting questions of what is a Jew, as in the case of Brother Daniel, a monk who demanded the right of entry, claiming that though converted to Christianity he was a Jew under the rabbinical definition—that is, a person born of a Jewish mother. The court rejected his claim, a decision that raised other interesting questions: Is Judaism a religion or, so to speak, a condition? Can a Jew, like Brother Daniel, abandon his religion and yet remain a Jew? He could, of course, have acquired Israeli citizenship after three years' residence, like any Moslem or Christian, but he wanted it as his right under the Law of Return. The doctrine established by his case may in the long run, as cases continue to arise, undergo a change. Perhaps some day that old question—What is a Jew?—may find an answer, although one thing is certain—if Israelis remain Jews, they will continue to dispute it.)

On July 30, 1961, the millionth immigrant since statehood arrived. Of these million, 431,000 came from Europe (beginning with 99,000 escapees and survivors from the concentration camps), with the largest groups coming from Romania and Poland: about 500,000 came from Asia and North Africa, including 125,000 from Iraq, 45,000 from Yemen, 33,000 from Turkey, others from Iran, India, and China, and 237,000 from Morocco, Tunisia, Libya, and Algeria. Thirteen thousand came from North and South America. The influx was never regular or planned, but came in waves or rushes in response to political crises and pressures. Airlifts brought the exodus from Iraq and Yemen under time deadline. Groups surged out from Poland and Romania, and a few from Russia, between sporadic liftings and lowerings of the Iron Curtain. In 1956, the number rose sharply in response to the revolt in Hungary and to the Suez campaign, which brought about the expulsion of 15,000–20,000 Jews from Egypt, many of them of the professional classes. Since 1961, another quarter of a million have come. Boats arrive at Haifa every week. Reception, examination, registration for first papers, arrangements for transportation and housing, and an initial grant of cash and food all take place on board. Every Jew admitted becomes a citizen with the vote at once; every non-Jew, once admitted, may become a citizen after three years' residence. It requires a visual effort of the imagination to picture what the settlement of almost 1.5 million strangers, nearly all requiring social and financial assistance, involves, not only physically in terms of housing, job-finding, adaptation, and schooling, but in the psychological strains on society and the tensions and frictions, both among the immigrants themselves and between them and the earlier residents. By contrast, the 500,000 Arab refugees of 1948, who have since doubled their number and remain an undigested lump and a charge on the U.N., could merge into the host countries with no barriers of language or custom, if the will to absorb them were present. Much of the cost of the operation in Israel, being beyond the powers of the state, is raised by contributions from Jews abroad and administered by a form of state within a state—the Jewish Agency. The origins, nature, and role of this remarkable institution, which is the residual office of the World Zionist Organization that virtually governed the Jews of Palestine under the Mandate, are complex, but it can be said that the work of the Agency for the time being is indispensable, while its implications are unresolved.

The effort on behalf of the immigrants is not of course purely eleemosynary. Israel needs these people to fill the vessel of the state. Besides filling the villages vacated by the Arabs in 1948, they create new settlements on land formerly non-arable. Twenty-one new towns and 380 new rural villages have been established since—and because—they began to arrive, and it is their increase of the manpower of Israel that now enables it to produce over three quarters of its own food as well as enough food exports to pay for the balance. The immigrants' labor is needed for defense purposes as well. The settlements are of every kind. Some are small, struggling communities with outhouses, weeds, and a few cows; others, multiple housing developments with streets, flung down on what was last month an empty hillside.

The greatest difficulty is providing income-producing work, especially among the Jews from North Africa, who despise manual labor—unlike the early European settlers, who idealized it and made it the cult of the kibbutz. Whereas they came to Palestine drawn by an ideal, the present Orientals have come as more or less passive victims of circumstance. To adapt at all, they must learn a new manner of living, a new language, how to read, and new agricultural or manual skills they never knew before, a task beyond the capacity of most of them. For teen-age immigrants, however, the period of military service, which provides as much classwork as drill, is an effective forcing house. Mixing with the native-born sabras, they learn to speak Hebrew and feel Israeli very soon.

Antagonism between Orientals and Europeans certainly exists. The latter, who led the return and reclaimed the country, have made Israel, despite geography, predominantly Western in ideas and habits. They are not particularly happy about the flood of darker-skinned people, whom they yearn to see balanced by a portion of their three million compatriots still locked up in Russia. (The Soviet government refuses to allow a general exit, because it would annoy their Arab friends and because voluntary departure would reflect poorly on the Soviet paradise.) The Orientals resent the fact that the earlier comers hold the better houses and jobs and, on the whole, the direction of the country (although there are two Cabinet ministers of Oriental origin). They are burdened with all the frustrations and troubles of a group which feels itself inferior. Israel has an integration problem, but it does not have a deep or hardened segregation pattern to overcome. With both will and need working for a rapid solution, Israelis talk of absorbing their Oriental citizens into the society within two generations.

Efforts are concentrated on the children, whose problems are many but whose inner transformation into Israelis can be quick and visible. When I visited a school in Beersheba, the woman principal, a Bulgarian by origin, showed me her classes with the pride of a creator, although the way had been rough. The absolutism of the Oriental father, particularly the Moroccan, collapses in Israel, she explained. The parents lose prestige, and the children, quickly feeling ashamed of them, look for revenge and become discipline problems. During her first year as a teacher, she said, her classes were so unruly that she cried every day for a year and wanted to quit, but her principal would not let her go. In a torrent of anguished reminiscence, she poured out all the difficulties of the past years, including, as an example of the immigrants' adjustment troubles, cases of stealing among children. When I suggested that this was not unknown in the private school my daughters attended in New York, not to mention every other American school I ever had any acquaintance with, she brushed aside the interruption, unimpressed. The problem is always bigger and better—or in this case, worse—in Israel.

As the teacher talked, the end-of-period bell rang, as it was doubtless doing all over the world. The corridors flooded with noisy youngsters, and the yard outside in the warm sun filled with groups kicking soccer balls. It could have been anywhere. The children all dressed much alike in slacks and colored shirts and cotton dresses, and one could not tell a Persian from a Pole or Moroccan from Hungarian.

Education is Israel's greatest internal task and absorbs the largest share, after defense, of the national budget. At the peak of the system stands the pride—or the wonder—of Israel: the reincarnated Hebrew University of Jerusalem. Opened in 1925, its original campus on Mt. Scopus, one of the eastern hills behind the Old City, was left inside Jordanian territory by the war of 1948, a loss that seemed almost as irreconcilable as the loss of the Wailing Wall. Under the terms of the truce the Israelis were to retain ownership and have access to the University and the adjoining Hadassah Hospital as a kind of enclave within Jordan, but as things have worked out, the only access that Jordan has permitted is a ritual inspection twice a month by Israeli officials in a sealed car escorted by the U. N. For a while after the war, classes were conducted in various buildings and rented premises, but the situation became too chaotic, and the hard decision to build a new home, giving up hope of regaining Mt. Scopus, had to be taken.

Begun in 1954 with money raised by Jews abroad, a new university has risen on the western edge of the city on a hill called Givat Ram. Accommodating over 10,000 students, it is a handsome complex of modern functional buildings whose straight lines contrast with the pool and curves and artful landscaping of a wide, open terrace. It seems to command its domain, but in fact the Hebrew University lives on impossibles, of which the chief, of course, is money. The government supplies a little over half its budget; tuition fees supply about one tenth; income from gifts another tenth; and the rest is a harassed look on the face of the president. While battling what is said to be the largest deficit of any university in the world, the Hebrew University runs because it must, as the pump of the intellectual and professional life of the country. Besides the undergraduate college, it operates professional schools of medicine, law, social work, agronomy, and education as well as a university press. Already overcrowded, its lecture halls stay open 13 hours a day to accommodate all classes. It can house, as yet, only a small proportion of students in dormitories, so the majority must find rented rooms in Jerusalem, which has a housing shortage. Most of them, in addition, must find full or part time employment to pay their way through. Out of the struggle come the skills the country needs.

Under the shadow of Arab enmity, Israel's need for friends and relationships with the outside world has drawn her into a program of quite surprising proportions that provides technical assistance to the underdeveloped countries. Last year, 832 Israeli technicians were serving in 62 countries, mostly in the emerging African states, but also in Burma, Ecuador, and other Asian and Latin American countries. They teach agriculture, irrigation, road construction, cost accounting, office management, and other essentials for a new country pulling itself into the modern stream. Students from the client countries—over 2,000 in 1965—come to Israel to learn on the job as well as to take academic courses at the university and professional schools. The flourishing program gives the Israelis immense satisfaction. It makes them feel they are putting back into the world the help they themselves have received, and it feeds their strong sense of mission. They are great improvers of mankind, and the noble sentiments expressed in the technical-assistance program are sometimes overpowering.

Of all enterprises to which Israel has been driven by need for an outlet to the world, the Red Sea port of Eilat is the most dramatic. Ten years ago it did not exist except as a name on the map and in the misty past as the Eziongeber of the Bible, where the people of Exodus halted on the flight from Egypt, and where later the Queen of Sheba disembarked. In 1949, when the first Israeli jeeps rolled in from the desert to occupy it, the only habitation was a deserted stone hut on the beach. Today Eilat is a functioning port for oceangoing ships, an airport, and a city of 13,000 with plans for expansion to 60,000. It might be Jack's Beanstalk except that human hands made it, not magic. Squeezed in between Egypt on the west and Jordan on the east, with the coast of Saudi Arabia below Jordan only four miles away, it sits on a seven-mile stretch of shoreline at the head of the Gulf of Aqaba. Only through this tiny slit could Israel open a door to the east and south for contact with the countries of Africa and the Orient. Although Eilat was allocated to Israel under the U. N. Partition plan of 1947, the right to use it had to be affirmed by force of arms, because Egypt blocked egress through the straits at the bottom of the Gulf. This was accomplished by the Sinai campaign of 1956, when, by taking possession of the land controlling the straits, Israel made their permanent opening a condition of the armistice which ended that adventure.

Given that development, Eilat burst like a racehorse from the starting gate. Its lifeline, the highway to Beersheba, was opened in 1958. As the artery of the Negev's future, the road has made possible the expansion of the desert and Dead

Sea chemical industries whose products, borne on diesel-powered, 50 ton trucks with eight pairs of wheels, now rumble into the docks of the new port. The port can accommodate four ships at the pier and three tankers at the oil jetty. Plans have been drawn up to double present capacity. Goods leave Eilat bound for Abyssinia, Iran, Burma, Singapore, Vietnam, Japan, and Australia. Rubber, imported from Singapore, is manufactured into tires at Petah Tikvah in the north, to be re-exported from Eilat to Iran as a finished product. The manager of the port is a young man of 24 who came to Eilat three years ago after his army service. To improve his command of English for dealing with shipmasters, he was going to England for two and a half months. Accustomed to government grants and the largesse of foundations, I asked who was sending him. "I send myself," he replied haughtily.

In addition to being a port, Eilat is booming as a tourist resort for sun-seekers and skin divers. It has 12 hotels of varying size and luxury; a tour by glass-bottomed boat to view the exotic fishes of the Red Sea; three museums, including a "musee de l'art moderne"; a library; an aquarium; a zoo; a park; a shopping plaza; a municipal hall of immodest proportions obviously designed for a town three times the present size; a 120 bed hospital under construction; two movie houses and a third under construction; a Philip Murray Community Center jointly established by the CIO and Histadrut, Israel's labor federation; two local airlines serving Tel Aviv, Haifa, and Beersheba; a bus line; three banks; three filling stations; two synagogues; two bars; and one mayor of dynamic capacity.

He is Joseph Levy, aged 43, a native of Egypt who in 1948 was arrested in Cairo as a Zionist youth leader and sent to a prison camp in the Sinai peninsula. Held there for a year, he planned an escape to the nearest point in Palestine, which happened to be Eilat, but was released before he could make the attempt. Reaching Israel, as it had now become, by way of Marseilles, he made for Eilat, having on the way talked himself into a job as manager of an airline branch office about to be opened there. He arrived in 1949, one of Eilat's Mayflower generation, and 10 years later was mayor.

A dark-haired, dark-skinned, quiet-mannered man, he wore when I saw him recently an air of enforced calm, as if he felt that were he to let himself go in reaction to all the demands, pressures, and harassments of his job, he might fly apart in a thousand pieces. He was entirely self-possessed, with the self-assurance that comes from having tackled and, if not solved, at least come through a chronic multiplicity of problems, and from acquiring the knowledge en route that no one of them need be fatal. Besides Hebrew and Arabic, he spoke English, French, and Italian, all of which he had been taught as a boy at the Jewish school in Cairo because, as the headmaster had explained to protesting parents, "Who knows today what may happen in the world? I must do what I can to prepare these children for anything."

Mayor Levy knew all about Mayor Lindsay of New York, kept similar hours, and left us after dinner to attend a meeting at 10:30. He had just been reelected for a second term by an increased majority and was supported by what he called a "wall-to-wall coalition" in the municipal council—that is, without other-party opposition on the council, a condition virtually unique in Israel. He ascribed it to the pioneers' sense of solidarity in Eilat. Out on the perimeter, too distant from the rest of the country to draw either water from the national carrier or electricity from the national grid, Eilat feels thrown on its own resources, a kind of fortress on the frontier.

The mayor recalled the hard early days when no one had any faith in the town's future. Businessmen would not invest capital there; no one would build a hotel until Histadrup put up the first; water would give out in the middle of a shower; power would fail. Families left after a few months, citing all sorts of reasons: schools were inadequate, hospitals nonexistent, provisions erratic, the summer's heat unbearable. "It was terrible to see them go." To keep at least the bachelors on the job, Histadrut was persuaded to build a girls' youth hostel ("We had to go to Histadrut for girls too"), but few girls came. Yet, bit by bit, with subsidies and from small beginnings, industry and tourism got started, gradually bringing in money, people, and developing facilities.

Water was, and remains, the major problem. Rainfall collected in cisterns, plus underground desert water that is too saline to be potable unless diluted by pure water, can together supply about 70 percent of requirements. The remaining 30 percent must be provided by desalinization, which, however uneconomic, the government subsidizes, since Eilat could not exist without it. Air conditioning makes an extra demand, but because of the extreme summer heat it is considered necessary in order to hold the population. The desalinization process is operated in conjunction with Eilat's independent power plant. Nearby, a second desalinization plant, using a refrigerating process, has proved ineffective. Mayor Levy shrugged when asked how water would be found to match the city's proposed expansion. "We can't let the water problem limit our plans," he said. "It will be found somehow." Perhaps he operated from some race memory of the water that gushed when Moses tapped the rock.

One alteration of nature already figured in his plans: to increase artificially the coastline available for tourist facilities by cutting a number of lagoons and canals inland from the sea, and eventually, to sell property along the banks of this "little Venice" for more hotels. The creeping shadow of Hilton could be felt over one's shoulder; already a Sheraton is being talked about. Doubtless in the course of that relentless advance, Eilat will one day become Israel's Miami. Such is progress.

Meanwhile, water or no water, Eilat plants as it builds. Fastgrowing eucalyptus trees already give shade and a green rest for the eye; shrubs and grass plots battle sand; scrawny saplings border a newly paved street, looking as if they had been planted yesterday. Waking early, I went for a walk before eight in the morning when the air was fresh, before the dust and heat would rise. A street cleaner on his knees was sweeping up the leftover dirt with a small brush, singing a melancholy Oriental chant while he worked. Over grass and shrubs, sprinklers were whirling as if no one had ever heard of a water shortage. They seemed symbols of the Israelis' refusal to accept limits, a living example of unlimited impossibility. In the sprinklers of Eilat, one could see what the professors call a "future-oriented society."

THE PROBLEMS OF RELIGION

TERENCE PRITTIE

It is probably surprising to some that there should be any "religious problem" at all in Israel, for, after all, isn't it a Jewish state? Yet, among the Jews of Israel there is striking conflict. There are those who are extremely Orthodox and others who wish to observe no ritual at all, and they seem to have a hard time adjusting to each other. In addition, there are Arab and Christian minorities in the country as well. In the following selection, Terence Prittie discusses the religious problems in the Jewish state.

On November 27, 1965, a long procession of more than a hundred cars wound its way slowly up the main road from Tel Aviv to Jerusalem. The road runs up hill and down dale, through forests planted in memory of the slain of the concentration camps, and nearer Jerusalem, through vineyards and gardens. This is a fairly busy road but normally peaceful enough, with only an occasional impatient driver sounding his horn. On this particular Saturday, the motorcade was halted two miles outside the city's boundaries at 11 A.M. by a solid posse of police, who blocked all four lanes of the highway and resolutely refused to let the cars go on.

Motorists climbed out of their cars, argued with the police, and went off to debate in little groups what their course of action should be. Half an hour after they had been halted, one of the drivers in the convoy lay down in the middle of the road; a dozen or so followed his example, and soon there were scores of people lying about the road, block-

Terence Prittie. "The Problem of Religion," *Israel: Miracle in the Desert.* New York: Frederick A. Praeger, Inc., 1967.

ing all traffic in or out of Jerusalem. It took the police three hours to remove the recumbent demonstrators and clear the road. It was mid-afternoon before the cars had dispersed; a dozen arrests were made.

The motorcade had been organized by the League Against Religious Coercion, and the intention of the demonstrators had been to drive through "secular" parts of Jerusalem in convoy in order to indicate their disapproval of religious organizations that, as they saw it, had been encroaching on the ordinary rights of the citizen. In particular, the demonstrators wanted to show their disapproval of the agreement of the City Council to close certain "religious" streets to all traffic on the Sabbath. This agreement had been approved by the recently appointed Mayor Teddy Kollek, one of the last people one would expect to make a compact with dyed-in-the-wool, traditionalist, religious groups.

Afterward, it was generally agreed that the police had prevented a much more serious disturbance. In Jerusalem, the young men and women of the religious groups had turned out in force to answer the challenge of the League Against Religious Coercion and were massed at various focal points in the city. There would have been a bloody melee in the midst of Jerusalem if the cars had driven through. Both sides meant business, and, as has happened before, Jews were ready to do battle with other Jews, utterly sure of the rightness of their cause.

The demonstrating members of the League Against Religious Coercion and the counterdemonstrators from the religious groups both represented extreme views in a nation that encourages freedom of religion and conscience. Israel in no way seeks to compel its citizens to carry out religious observances. All religious denominations are free to worship in their own way, and their leaders freely cooperate with the Ministry of Religious Affairs. Religious toleration is rightly regarded as particularly important by a people that has suffered so much from religious and racial persecution.

Officially, the 2.25 million Jews of Israel all belong to the Jewish faith, with the exception of the small minorities of 5,000 Keraites, who accept only the literal law of the Bible, and a few hundred Samaritans, who have larger communities in neighboring Jordan and who reject some of the teachings of the Bible. The 200,000 Muslims of Israel form a single religious community, while the 60,000 Christians are split into Greek Catholics, Greek Orthodox, Roman Catholics, Maronites, and Protestants. There are also around 30,000 Druses, whose forefathers broke away from Islam in the eleventh century and who make an annual pilgrimage to the tomb of Jethro, the father-in-law of Moses.

In Israel, religion is not, as in many Protestant and Catholic countries, divorced from everyday life. Members of the religious groups fall under the authority of their clergy in all matters of personal status, and, for the laity, the supreme religious authority, the Chief Rabbinate—consisting of an Ashkenazi and a Sephardi Chief Rabbi and the Rabbinical Council, which supervises the eight regional rabbinical courts—have complete authority in such day-to-day matters as marriage, divorce, and burial; there are no civil marriage ceremonies in Israel. Israelis individually and as a community are brought into constant contact with the religious authorities—whether they like it or not. The Jewish holy days are observed nationally; as a government publication poetically explains, the Sabbath and other festivals "are part of the air" the people of Israel breathe. The nearly 5,000 synagogues of Israel are generally full. The synagogue, of course, is more than a place of worship; it is a meeting place for the whole community, where there is much sober discussion of secular as well as religious problems.

The Sabbath and Jewish festivals are official holidays, but Sunday is the day of rest for the Muslim and Christian minorities. All Muslim, as well as Jewish, clergy are paid by the state, and the state provides religious education for Jewish children between the ages of five and fourteen whose parents want it for them. One out of every three Jewish children is educated at a religious institution. But the proportion of the population that can be regarded as strictly Orthodox —regularly attending the synagogue on the Sabbath, regularly studying the Bible, the Mishna (a compendium of scholarly religious evaluations and records), and the Talmud, strictly obeying the Mosaic dietary and other laws, and strictly applying the ethical standards set out in the Bible to everyday life, and accepting a high degree of discipline and devotion—is smaller.

Jerusalem is, as one might expect, the center of organized religion in Israel. It contains around 400 synagogues and the Chief Rabbinates of the Sephardi and Ashkenazi communities. Religious groups regard Jerusalem not only as their capital but to some extent as their own domain. They are dispersed throughout the city but are especially strongly entrenched in the Mea Shearim quarter, in the north of the city and close to the boundary of Jordan and the sole entrance into Jordanian territory, the Mandelbaum Gate.

Mea Shearim is an area of twisting alleys and rambling roads, many of them unpaved and dusty. Some of its houses still lie in the ruins created in the fighting in 1948. On the Sabbath, Mea Shearim is an oasis of quiet in a still fairly animated city. Sometimes signs are hung across the streets of Mea Shearim telling the daughters of Israel to dress and behave with becoming modesty. In the streets, you will find a few groups of small boys playing the Israeli version of hopscotch, with a dignified restraint and little laughter, and small girls skipping rope in silence. From some of the houses come sounds of singing or of intoning of prayers. Members of the religious communities walk through the narrow lanes purposefully, with their white stockings, black velvet and silk robes, and imposing brown fur hats. Sometimes they have their sons with them, with skullcaps on their heads, shaven save for the long side-curls. These are not the equivalent of Sunday strollers, but men walking with a purpose:

to the synagogue, to a private prayer meeting, or to a Bible reading.

Just outside the well-defined boundaries of Mea Shearim, motorists whirl down the Yaffo Road, on their way to picnicking places in the country. In the Yaffo Road, the usual animated groups discuss the football prospects, and teams of boys play basketball in the courtyards of otherwise deserted schools. Outside Mea Shearim, the Sabbath is coming progressively more and more secularized.

The Jew, it seems, will often take an extreme view in order later to be able to compromise. But this is not the case with the controversions, which are becoming steadily more bitter in Israel, between the religious communities and the spearheads of secular opposition to them. With some reason and with whatever right goes with possession, the religious communities regard Mea Shearim as their preserve, but in their efforts to maintain the sanctity of the Sabbath they have extended their activities well beyond the easily defined boundaries of their own district. Thus, the pretext for the demonstration of the League Against Religious Coercion was the Sabbath closing of the Rehov Balfour, which is not in the Mea Shearim at all. It was, perhaps, only a coincidence that Chief Rabbi Nissim, of the Sephardi community, lived on that particular street. But its closure seemed to be an arbitrary action on the part of the Mayor, who had found it politic to make this concession to his colleagues from the religious parties on the City Council.

Only a short time before, the religious communities of Jerusalem had forced the closure of a youth club opened near the Jordanian border with the excellent object of keeping young people off the streets. They gave two reasons for their objection to the club: it was for both boys and girls, which was contrary to their own rules; and it was "too near" an Orthodox religious quarter of the city. They had staged demonstrations in the northwestern suburbs of Jerusalem early in the Sabbath mornings in order to prevent busloads of people leaving for a day by the sea near Tel Aviv. They had protested furiously against a municipal swimming pool because women were allowed in the pool at the same time as men. On various occasions, younger members of the religious communities have stoned motorists for driving close to Orthodox quarters on the Sabbath. (One of their more recent targets was a coach-load of astonished Spanish pilgrims.) In 1964, the stone-throwing turned into a formidable riot, when barriers were erected in the Rehov Shivtei Yisrael in order to stop tourists coming into the city from the Mandelbaum Gate. Scores of police had to be called out, and there was a pitched battle before the barriers could be cleared.

In October, 1963, there were equally wild scenes in the so-called Hungarian section of Mea Shearim, where a group of Jews from Hungary settled in the 1920's, organized by the religious extremists of the group that calls itself Neturei Karta (Guardians of the City). The police were greeted with cries of "Gestapo!" and "Nazis!" and the nearby offices of the Ministry of Education were attacked. A ripple of this riot reached across the Atlantic. Sympathetic New York Jews, under the leadership of a Rabbi Joel Teitelbaum, staged a protest march in support of Neturei Karta and daubed swastikas on the offices of the Israeli Consulate General.

According to the Talmud, there is no purpose in a Jew debating doctrinal matters with a Jewish nonbeliever, since argument will only make the latter deny and ridicule Holy Scriptures all the more. (He may debate doctrine with a Gentile to his heart's content.) This certainly seems to have been the view of the religious communities on a number of occasions, since they have operated with sticks, stones, and noisy imprecations rather than with arguments and with recourse to due processes of law. Yet, the religious communities have usually lost the immediate engagement. Busloads of Jerusalem's citizens continue to speed out to the seaside on the Sabbath; the municipal swimming pool is filled with swimmers on every warm day; and tourists are not usually molested on their way to or from the Mandelbaum Gate. In 1965, the sole victory of the religious communities was outside Jerusalem, in Ashdod, where they succeeded in stopping Sabbath work-shifts in the harbor by standing under cranes and sitting on the hoods of trucks.

The Israeli government formed in January, 1966, was confronted, however, with one problem that was a direct legacy of the religious controversies. Prime Minister Eshkol was forced to include the National Religious Party in his broadly based coalition. This and the two other religious parties wanted a law passed to regularize Sabbath observances; in particular, they wanted to ban all public transport on the Sabbath everywhere, including the city of Haifa, which had previously been regarded as a "mixed" Jewish-Arab community where public transport was permitted on the Sabbath, and to classify as public transport and ban the rapid and inexpensive Sherut taxi services. The National Religious Party, in addition, wanted two extra hours of religious instruction required at the primary schools maintained by religious groups—attended by about a third of Israel's eight-to-fourteen-year olds. Finally, the party considered that the Chief Rabbinate should be the court of appeal for all cases concerning the laws governing Orthodox dietary regulations.

A tug-of-war within the new government was certain, for its left-wing elements were not prepared to tolerate any of these proposed changes and did not want a Sunday observance law at all. They have pointed out that previous legislation merely laid down that the Sabbath was a day of rest and left municipal and local councils to decide what regulations should be enforced. This has led to widely conflicting practices. In some places, certain forms of stage entertainment are allowed on the Sabbath. There is no uniformity about restaurants staying open. There are buses only at

Haifa, but Sheruts everywhere; with some reason, the opponents of stricter regulations have pointed out that the banning of Sheruts would affect the less well-to-do, since people with more money have their own cars, and there can be no question of trying to interfere with their freedom of movement. The "anti-coercionists" point out, too, that religious Jews are trying to get the best of both worlds—seeking to enforce strict regulations while continuing to benefit from the work done on the Sabbath by those who man electricity, gas, and other essential public services.

Maurice Samuel has written, "The Jewish people loves and hates itself, admires and despises itself, with pathological intensity. It is either God-selected or God-rejected."[1] There is a painful element of truth in this statement. The religious groups, for instance, denounced Uri Avneri, an independent member of the 1966 Knesset, as "the Canaanite" and accused him of trying to "organize a pogrom" because he sided with the League Against Religious Coercion. Liberals, for their part, ridiculed the religious groups as fossils and fanatics with no regard for the opinions and rights of the majority and no understanding of practical democracy. Ben-Gurion, with his usual individualistic outlook—for his religious convictions have never prevented him from criticizing fanaticism and espousing the cause of the temporal against the religious authority whenever he saw fit to do so—had his own word to say about the religious and the nonreligious: "To the ultra-orthodox, a Jew in America who prays every morning is a better Jew than the one who comes to Israel and does not attend synagogue. I believe that any Jew who lives in Israel, the Land of Zion, is a more religious Jew than the most pious Jew who *can* come to Israel and does *not.* (Ben-Gurion had a sneaking fellow feeling for religious zealots all the same, because they "looked like one's own grandfather," and it was simply not possible to "slap one's grandfather into jail.")

1. Chaim Weizmann, *A Biography by Several Hands,* eds. M. Weisgal and J. Carmichael (New York: Atheneum, 1963).

Yet, a great many Israelis cannot regard the religious zealots so tolerantly. They believe that their fanaticism has driven many Israelis away from the synagogue and encouraged them to declare themselves agnostics openly. They think that the fanatics make religion a burden, almost a joke, and that they are a handicap to the state.

They cite the example of the Neturei Karta group. This small group, consisting of only a few hundred families, most of them living in Mea Shearim, have made up for lack of numbers by violence, and they have directed their attacks often at the Chief Rabbinate and other religious bodies. In 1921, indeed, they demanded a day of fasting and penance because a Chief Rabbinate had been formed; they have made violent and vicious attacks on it time after time and have rejected its right to frame the regulations for ritual slaughter (shehita). They denounced the enfranchisement of women and many other progressive political measures, and they opposed Zionism and the establishment of a secular state of Israel. They even refused to help in any way in the efforts to bring the victims of Nazi concentration camps out of Europe to Israel.

Neturei Karta believes in the totality of Divine Providence. Its view is that Jews must accept their fate on earth whatever it may be, do nothing to help themselves, and wait for the ultimate act of God, the sending of the Messiah to the world. According to this group's interpretation of Torah, the Law, it is prohibited for Israel to have any form of Jewish government, for the establishment of the secular state would weaken and finally destroy the godly life of suffering of the Jewish people. Of the first government of Israel, Neturei Karta stated, "We openly declare that we do not recognize the regime of blasphemers; we do not accept their authority; and we do not bow to their rule. We are in no way bound by their laws and directives."

Neturei Karta is, of course, the most extreme manifestation of Orthodoxy in Israel. In general, the majority of Orthodox Jews speak a very different language and are completely loyal to the state of Israel. But Orthodox Jews nevertheless show a strong disinclination to move with the times. They insist not only on the strict observance of the Laws of Moses, but on the early Biblical interpretation of those laws. A case in point is provided by the dietary laws governing "kosher" food.

These laws lay down that certain foods may not be eaten or may not be eaten in conjunction with other foods.[2] Thus, meat and dairy products may not be eaten together, and there must be an interval of at least four hours between eating beef, say, and butter. All livestock should be ritually slaughtered, which simply means that the maximum amount of blood must be drained from the carcass and certain parts removed from it and thrown away (these include the "lights," but not the liver and kidneys). This draining of blood from the carcass probably helps to account, incidentally, for the gray and tasteless meat that kosher restaurants usually seem to serve. Any form of seafood that has no scales should not be eaten at all. Nor should pork; the pig is an animal that is reviled throughout Jewish history. (Pork is not a political issue in Israel today. The breeding of pigs by Jewish farmers is forbidden, and the ban is observed, but they can be bred by Arab farmers, and pork and bacon are sold up to the outskirts of the markets of Tel Aviv and Jerusalem.)

The question why Moses laid down these laws is not asked by Orthodox Jews; their view is that the dietary laws of the Biblical era were established for purposes of hygiene

2. One curiosity produced by dietary laws has been the controversy over whether whisky is kosher. The Rabbinate has been unhappy about the import of whisky, which may have been matured in sherry casks—in which case it ranks as "wine" or the "fruit of the vine," and as such, must not be drunk by Orthodox Jews. A suggestion was made to the Scottish Council for Development and Industry that whisky firms might like to allow a measure of rabbinical supervision of the production of Scotch so that imports into Israel would not be liable to a rabbinical ban. Blandly, the Scottish Council pointed out that the blending of whisky was a trade secret and that the presence of a rabbi, however devout, would not conform with established practice.

in those times, but much more important, imposed a discipline of selectivity in diet and sobriety in eating that is still relevant. Orthodox Jews, indeed, consider that the Mosaic laws cannot be questioned but only accepted and fulfilled.

Another problem is the law of Shemittah, under which all land must lie fallow every seventh year beginning at the festival of Rosh Hashanah in early autumn. Exodus tells us, God ordered Moses: "Six years thou shalt sow thy land, and shalt gather in the fruits thereof: But the seventh year thou shalt let it rest and lie still." This regulation originally made good sense. Pastoral peoples who settled down to farming were apt to try to take too much out of the land while putting nothing back. But in the middle of the twentieth century, the idea of leaving land fallow is nonsensical. How are farms, including the big enterprises of the kibbutzim, to function if production must be halted every seventh year? Orthodox Israeli agriculturalists have devised ways of defeating Shemittah. They have fenced off corners of fields to lie symbolically fallow on behalf of the whole farm. They have gone to even greater pains and created small paddocks, systematically grazed for six years and then given a "rest year." Some farmers cover their tractors with worn-out army camouflage nets every seventh year, for according to one rabbinical interpretation, the planting in the seventh year is legal if it is done under an enclosure. In a great many cases, Jewish farmers have simply transferred their land, on the seventh year, to an accommodating Arab. The Arab deposits a small sum of money, which he will reclaim—along with a small "tip"—when the year ends. A deed of sale and of repurchase is "legalized." A sacred law has not been infringed.

The dietary laws, Shemittah, and the like can give a false impression of the role of religion in Israel. It might be assumed that outdated practices and the invasion of politics by a number of religious parties, reveal a purely negative impact of the religious communities. This is not the case.

During the two thousand years of exile of the Jewish

people, the Bible has been a solid and enduring source of inspiration and a solace in suffering. Whenever in doubt or distress, the "people of the Book" have had the Bible to fall back on and its assurances that the Jews are God's chosen people and that between God and Abraham was a covenant that would last as long as time itself. How vastly important was this covenant!

The religion of the Jews has another unique and important aspect: it created an all-embracing sense of community.

> Judaism is the religion of a community, because essential concerns of the religion itself are communal. It emphasizes as much as any Protestant Church the ultimate responsibility of each individual for his destiny before God, yet it is not a religion basically concerned with individual salvation. It believes in the divine society as much as any Christian of the Catholic tradition; but it regards this divine society not primarily as a body of believers separate from the larger ethnic or national community in which they live, but as the national unit itself. . . . The place which the Church occupies in Christian thought is occupied in Judaism by the whole people, good, bad, and indifferent, faithful and unfaithful. Christianity, even before St. Augustine, thought in terms of two cities, the City of God, and a city of this world whose ruler was not God. Judaism knows no such dualism.[3]

The children of Israel believed themselves to be a community devoted to the fulfillment of a divine purpose. The Jews believed in the restoration of that community which had joined in its covenant with God. The Return, in fact, may not have seemed as miraculous to the Jews as it did to the rest of the world. And the desire to return to the promised land was fortified by the Messianic hope, which could

3. James Parkes, *Five Roots of Israel* (London: Valentine, Mitchell and Co., 1966), p. 7.

only visualize the Messiah coming to His own, in His own time, at the appointed and only possible place—Zion-Jerusalem. The Bible, and the religion bound up with it, have produced that faith "which moves mountains." Without the Bible, the foundation of the state of Israel in 1948 would have been inconceivable.

The most vital adjunct to the Bible has been the Hebrew language, which survived throughout the two thousand years of the Dispersion as the language of the priesthood, of history, and of the elite. In the Hebrew language, too, was the germ of the deathless idea of Jewish nationhood. Two of the most indispensable architects of the new Israel were Moses Hess, the first to write, in the 1860's, of a Jewish territorial resettlement of the Holy Land, and Eliezer Ben-Yehuda, who produced five volumes of his Hebrew dictionary before he died in 1922. (His work was only completed in 1959 with the publication of the sixteenth and last volume of the dictionary.) The dictionary, too, was in its way a miracle, for what other ancient language has been rescued and renewed in this way? In Ireland, Erse has remained the language of the schoolroom and, on occasion, of the Dublin Parliament, but contributed only little to the Irish national revival; Hebrew was, next to the Bible itself, the most formative agent in developing the Israeli national idea. And the Rabbinate played the biggest part in keeping the Hebrew language alive.

The practical application of religion in daily life can be seen at any of the religious kibbutzim. One, which I have visited, at Yavneh, south of Tel Aviv, is affiliated with the National Religious Party. The kibbutz more than pays its way, with mixed farming and the biggest chicken hatcheries in Israel. Its inhabitants work hard, eat plain but wholesome food, enjoy sports, cinema, and concerts as their principal recreations, allow themselves radios, phonographs, and books as their only "luxuries." Here, where a thousand people are living and working, life goes on in very much the same way as in other kibbutzim. But there is, naturally, a marked accent on religion. Religious instruction takes up a quarter of the time in the schoolrooms, but does not interfere with the general education of the children, whose standards are probably higher than in most secular kibbutzim—given the teachers' extreme dedication and the pupils' high degree of discipline. There are regular prayers, and special Bible readings and lectures on religious subjects on the Sabbath. On Friday evening, candles are lit at sunset; then follows a service for all but the infants in the synagogue, rounded off by communal singing. The evening meal is blessed and is followed by prayers and singing. Everyone goes early to bed and rises early on the Sabbath for a two-hour service. Breakfast is a solemn meal, with grace said over a dedicatory glass of wine. There is another service at noon; otherwise, the day is spent in rest and reflection and in visits between families. At sunset on the Sabbath, the first fire for twenty-four hours is kindled.

The laws of the Sabbath are exactly observed. Not even the switches for regulating the heat in the chicken hatcheries may be touched on the Sabbath, and a reserve generator has now been installed with a self-regulator. Previously, Yavneh lost up to a thousand dollars a year as a result of shorts in the electricity system and chicks dying for lack of warmth. Even now, little may be done on the Sabbath for a sick animal, for the veterinary surgeon may not be fetched from outside the kibbutz. If a swarm of locusts descends on Yavneh's fruit trees on the Sabbath, they may not be driven away. Children and adults who injure themselves may only have their wounds bandaged in the simplest way unless there is an obvious danger of infection. The food served on the Sabbath is cooked the day before and reheated. Washing up is restricted to placing dirty dishes in a vat full of water and disinfectant. There are no sports on the Sabbath and no music save the organized singing.

It is difficult to come to any conclusions about the religious problems of Israel. One can only note with alarm that the religious and nonreligious communities are drifting farther apart as time goes on and that there exists an increasing urge on the part of the nonreligious to declare themselves as agnostic or even atheistic. The religious controversy affects the strength and cohesion of the community as a whole. But reform must come from the Rabbinate and not from the state, which does not dare to interfere with Rabbinical law and practice. And for the Rabbinate, one thing should be clear: organized religion cannot retreat into a spiritual fastness, where men in the street cannot and will not follow.

IN THE FOOTSTEPS OF THE PAST

AUBREY MENEN

Israel is a land where the people have made ancient history co-exist with history in the making. The Israel antiquity law, for instance, requires that when a builder strikes an archeological find, engineers must halt construction until the merit of the find can be determined.

In this way, as Aubrey Menen points out in the next chapter, the Bible is turned into a living document.

My first night in Jerusalem was rather like a Homeric banquet. When we had eaten and drunk, my Israeli friends told me long stories of what they had done in the Six Days' War. It had finished only two months earlier, and they were still bursting with its excitement. Beside all this, my own mission seemed pallid. I had come to visit the shrines and monuments of Israel, and it seemed I had chosen just the wrong time. But one of my friends, after bidding me good night, turned back to say: "Go and see Rachel's tomb. I think you'll see something to surprise you."

So I rose early next morning and drove southward out of Jerusalem, past the rubble of war into the peace of the countryside, until I came to a cluster of low white houses. The car drew up beside one that looked smaller than the rest. A tired young soldier sat on a stool at the entrance. "Hat," he said, yawning. Then, seeing I had none, he reached into a box and brought out a little black skullcap made of paper. I

Aubrey Menen. "In the Footsteps of the Past," *Holiday* Magazine (December, 1967).

perched it on the top of my head, and the young soldier's face lit up with a beautiful smile. My driver shifted it to the back of my head, where it should go, and, somewhat embarrassed, I went into the house.

There was one large room with whitewashed walls, unadorned save for a faded banner. In the middle was a large box made of stone, taller than a man, with a curved top. It looked very like an enormous trunk such as the Victorians used, but a trunk for a traveling giant. It was freshly painted in battleship gray. There was nothing on it, whatever—not a name, not a flower, not a carving. I stared at it, for there was nothing else to look at. I suspected my Israeli friend of having made a joke at my expense.

I searched my memory. There was something I had known about Rachel, but in that bare room with the soldier at the door, it would not come to mind.

Suddenly there was the sound of many voices outside. The soldier got to his feet. "Quiet!" he said. "This is a holy place. Behave yourselves."

Then through the narrow door filed a procession of men and women of all ages and with them some children. As they came into the room and saw the tomb, they fell silent. A motherly woman ran to it. She stretched out her arm and embraced one corner of it. Then she kissed it, not with the light kiss of a Catholic kissing a relic, but passionately again and again, with tears. A tall young man dressed all in black, with long ringlets falling down his cheeks, took out a small, worn book with Hebrew characters. He raised his voice in a loud chant, and the others, now packing the room, joined him in the prayer. I listened, pressed against the wall, and as the rolling sound of the Hebrew echoed on my ears my memory awoke. I spoke to myself:

> *"A voice was heard in Ramah, lamentation and bitter weeping: Rachel weeping for her children refused to be comforted for her children, because they were not."*

They were the words of the Prophet Jeremiah, and whenever I heard them as a boy, I had been deeply moved, for they seemed to me the loveliest words in the English language.

Now another man with a book raised his voice, and he too lamented, rocking backward and forward in front of the tomb, the little book held high, his voice keening through a long series of half notes of infinite sadness.

The group moved around the tomb, touching it, kissing it, stroking its cold surface with affectionate hands, until all had made the full circuit. Then, with eyes shining, they filed out into the sunlight.

I went out behind the last of them. He was a tall youngster, burned brown by the sun. I judged him to be a worker on a kibbutz, because he wore their economical dress—a pointed cap, a shirt so light it is almost a vest, small shorts, and sandals. He, in turn, eyed my tropical suit.

"Shalom," I said.

"Shalom," he replied.

"My suit was made in Rome," I said. "I don't like it. I'm going to wear it out."

"I like it," he said. He spoke in school-taught English, but it served. "One day we shall all have suits like that in Israel."

"You work on a kibbutz?"

"No. I am a student now. But soon." He made the chopping-off gesture with his hand that is universal throughout the Mediterranean among the young.

"Soon you're going to be a soldier," I said.

He nodded.

"What do you study?"

"History."

"Ancient? Modern?"

"*Israeli* history," he said with emphasis.

We were walking slowly toward the truck that had brought him. It was fitted with rough wooden seats that were already filled with his companions. They began signaling to him to hurry up.

"Tell me," I said. "Is that really Rachel's tomb?"

"Of course. It is mentioned in the Bible during the time of the Kings. It had a column then."

"And is Rachel there?"

"Maybe. One day we take spades and dig." He threw an amused glance at one of the men with long ritual ringlets. He winked at me and held his finger to his lips. "But not yet. Shalom." He ran lithely to the truck and climbed aboard as it was moving off. Its place was immediately taken by a new arrival, and this was followed by another and another until I counted ten of them. From each poured Israelis bent on visiting the dull gray stone that had suddenly been brought to life for me.

I drove on to Hebron. Here, in what may well be one of the oldest cities in the world, I saw the same thing I had seen at Rachel's tomb, but on a scale that was, at first, frightening. A vast space had been cleared, as big, perhaps, as a third of the whole town. It was jammed with buses, trucks, cars, and motorcycles, which sweating policemen were trying to reduce to some working order. From these streamed group after group of Israelis, shouting, singing, laughing, or talking at the top of their voices. They formed a continuous column, that made its way on foot through a long, narrow road. On either side, ham to ham, squatted Arabs selling trinkets, sweetmeats, ices, cold drinks, postcards, coffee from tall metal urns, and handwoven Bedouin cloth. At one point, a camel, magnificently attired in a bright saddle cloth, bells, and colored ropes, sat by its Bedouin master, who offered the Israelis a ride. Jews bought freely, but no Jew sold. In 1929, they had been massacred, and those who survived left Hebron, not to return until now, after the Six Days' War, when Hebron suddenly had become Jewish again. This vast throng was visiting, with great joy, the city of Abraham, of

Isaac, and of Sarah, the town where David was anointed king and Absalom rebelled against his father.

They wound through the bazaar until the road became a path of steps that led up a hill of yellow rocks. On top, so mighty that it seemed part of the hill itself, was a great castle with battlements, grim but beautiful against the clear blue sky of Israel. The path of steps turned into a great stone staircase, but I let the crowd go past me. I stood and stared at the castle in wonder and reverie, for below it lay the cave that Abraham had bought from Ephron, the Hittite, as a grave for his wife Sarah.

Abraham's chaffering with him was all recorded in the Bible, as I well knew, for I had been made to learn its details in my Scripture class at school. I had learned them, got my passing marks, and had thought no more about Abraham until now, when I stood among these people who were his descendents and who rejoiced in the fact.

We all moved up the steps, went in under a great arch, and found ourselves in a many-sided hall, low-roofed and plain. To one side was a recess behind a grille, with a tomb like that of Rachel but covered with an embroidered pall, faded with age. This was the cenotaph of Abraham. Opposite, under a similar pall, lay that of Sarah. There was no chance of kissing them. They could be seen only through iron bars, and some Israelis touched these reverently. Others gazed or prayed. One woman, poorly dressed and with a lined face, stared at Abraham's cenotaph for a while and then said: "But Sarah—where is Sarah?" Others pointed to the other side of the hall, and with an extraordinary expression of joy and welcome, she ran across the hall, spread her arms to grasp the railings, looked at the cenotaph, nodded her head, and smiled, as though she was meeting someone she had once known well and was seeing again after a long, long time.

We came out; we passed again through the bazaar; we

ate, drank, chattered, and joked. Everybody was happy except the camel, which gave rides and did a roaring business in a thoroughly bad temper. These pilgrimages, this elation, are new in Israel, and it is good that this has happened, for I have seen how it was before.

One morning I left my hotel in Jerusalem, picked my way through the Old City, and after being several times lost, found my way to the Wailing Wall. The Wall formed one side of a gigantic piazza. At its foot, dwarfed by its immensity, were black-clad figures, the men divided from the women by an iron partition. There was a sound of chanting, not very loud. The mourners faced the Wall, sometimes touching it, but mostly holding prayer books. There was no theatricality. I had expected something like the professional mourning women of Sicily, who are unnerving in their wails and tears. But here all is somber and dignified. Not everyone prays. Groups stand about, talking, like people on a church porch.

Those at the Wall were mourning for the destruction of the Temple and the loss of Israel by the Jews. They have done so for centuries. But now Israel is home again; Jerusalem belongs to it once more, and I did not speak to a Jew or an Arab who seriously thought that Israel would let it go again.

I left the Wall and went to see the young Israelis respectfully taking off their shoes at the entrance to the Dome of the Rock, a Muslim shrine, which stands on the site of the Temple, and hear them talking in whispers in its stupendous rotunda. They come, I was told, in their thousands. This may not be a better thing to do, but there is hope in it. Jerusalem, for me, is a city too full of old despairs.

The rock that the Dome covers is a huge mass of stone from which, so Muslims believe, Muhammad took off on a journey to Heaven. The building resembles a mosque without minarets. We do not know who the architect was, but he created that rarest of buildings, one in which the proportions are perfect. To avoid making it look correct but dull, he smothered both inside and out with decoration, so that the shrine is ablaze with precious marbles, gilding and mosaics—green, blue, gold, even mother-of-pearl. The soaring dome is covered inside with an intricate fretwork of moldings, painted in a variety of dazzling colors that we would now call psychedelic.

From this place sacred to the Prophet of the Sword, I journeyed to a shrine of the Prince of Peace. I went to see the Church of the Nativity, at Bethlehem. Its front is smaller than that of a New England parish church—at least, what can be seen of it today. It has no door. You enter through a tunnel so low you have to bend almost double. Inside is a nave lined with pillars, which have been there since the time of the Roman Emperor Constantine, and surrounded by walls so dilapidated that it would seem that no repairs have been done since. Like the Holy Sepulcher in Jerusalem, the church is controlled by more than one sect. Greek Orthodox priests are in charge of the church, but Franciscans control some underground shrines in the basement. Again, as in the Sepulcher, the various priests live in anything but Christian friendship.

I saw one Franciscan standing in a doorway and I asked him where I could go down to the grotto of the Nativity. He pointed to a door under the high altar, which was, at that moment, completely surrounded by Orthodox priests in full canonicals, swinging censers. I was puzzled, but I obediently went. I found myself in the middle of the celebration of Holy Communion. An irate priest barked at me (and with reason). A bearded sacristan seized my shoulder and yanked me up some steps, while the Franciscan, who was the cause of it all, regarded the scene with other-worldly calm.

My shoulder hurt for a while, but I was quite proud of the fact. For centuries, the factions of priests in the Church of the Nativity have tried to put a spoke in one another's wheels, even to the point of causing riots. My little incident seemed to me to have a fine patina of age.

But when, at last, the priests were gone and I could go down into the grotto, I found all was tranquil. Unlike the Holy Sepulcher, the place does not raise doubts. The Church of the Holy Sepulcher was razed by a mad caliph. We must believe that this caliph, having taken the trouble to tear down the church, left the tomb standing. He may, of course, have done so; the Sepulcher may be genuine. On the other hand, it could be a pious fake. But this cave in Bethlehem was reverenced by Christians as far back as a mere hundred and thirty years after the death of Christ. Jerome, a scholar as well as one of the earliest Fathers of the Church, had so few doubts about its being genuine that he retired to live beside it.

The grotto is small, with most of the original rock still showing. In one niche is an altar. Underneath it on the natural stone is a star of silver gilt, with an inscription saying that here Jesus was born of the Virgin Mary. When I went down into the cave, it was empty save for one Christian, praying on his knees. There is no splendor or pomp. There are some hanging lamps, covered in soot, a small mosaic, too blackened to be seen. That is all, and that is as it should be. I was deeply moved. I doubt the shepherds, I doubt their star and I do not believe in the Magi at all, but I do believe that Jesus of Nazareth was born here in a manger—and if it is true that there are angels, surely it was a time for singing.

There are grottoes, too, at Nazareth. One is presented as the site of the Annunciation, another as the House of the Virgin; and there are even some old foundations that someone in the 17th Century decided was Joseph's workshop. These have to be looked at with the eye of faith. I followed the example of the founder of Christianity and left Nazareth for Capernaum.

It was here that Jesus taught, and it is here that the

modern believer should come, because he can believe what he sees. The Capernaum of Christ is no more than a mound beside the Sea of Galilee. But down by the shore is a ruin that set me dreaming. There are some white columns standing among eucalyptus trees and a scatter of carved stones. These are the remains of the synagogue. What I saw before me was built three centuries after the death of Christ, but it was built on the site of the synagogue in which he preached. Beneath my feet lay the remains of the building that was paid for and given to the Jews by a Roman centurion who loved them, the man about whom Jesus said, marveling: "I say unto you, I have not found so great faith, no, not in Israel."

This, indeed, is a holy place and so is the hill that rises behind Capernaum. It is not very high. It has two summits joined by a saddle, and it was here that Jesus taught those tremendous paradoxes that we know as the Beatitudes. It is a quiet place. The Sea of Galilee, changing color like a chameleon, lies in front of you. It is not difficult to conjure up the preacher, in his long gown and turban (Jesus wore one, like everybody else), and the crowd, intent, puzzled, and waiting for one of those miracles they had heard so much talk about.

There is only one other place as evocative as this, and that is the Mount of Olives at Jerusalem. It is austere; it has a scattering of trees on it—not olives, but the somber cypress. At its foot lies a garden called Gethsemane. Inevitably, it is cared for to the point of primness. There is a church, but a discreet one, and some ancient olives of endless age. In the evening, when the pilgrims have gone, there is silence and the long shadows that prelude the coming of night. Watching them, my thoughts turned to that other night that forever sums up the agony of mankind; the pain of having to live, and having to die.

Lastly I went into the desert, down to the Dead Sea, to see something as sad as Gethsemane and as terrible. It is a flat-topped mountain that rises above the plain where once stood Sodom and Gomorrah. It is called Masada, and in the days of the Roman conquest, it was a fortress. When the Romans sacked and partially destroyed Jerusalem, almost a thousand Jews retreated to this fastness—men, women, and children—to defy the conqueror to the last. They did not know what end they would make. They only knew that they would never give in.

The Romans followed them and besieged them. They built a ramp up the side of the mountain—a ramp that was a mountain in itself and can still be seen, towering over the ruins of their encampment. They hauled their siege engines up it and began to batter down the walls.

The Jews gathered themselves together. A decision was made. Ten men were picked by lot, and this band went among the men, the women, and their children, killing them with their swords, with their full consent.

At last only the ten men were left. These took torches, and gathering their possessions together, they set them on fire. But they left the food in the storehouses intact, as a message to the Romans—they had not done this thing because they were starving; they had done it because they were determined to remain free, even if dying were the only way they could be so.

The ten men now drew lots. One of them was chosen, and he killed all nine of his companions. Then he took his own sword, and he fell upon it.

When the Romans broke through the breach, they found a silent fort and more than 900 dead people. Only two women and some children to tell the story. It is recorded that the Romans did not, as was their custom, rejoice at their victory.

At the Feast of the Passover, tens of thousands of Israelis face the steep climb up to the summit of Masada and stand among the ruins. There they silently vow that Masada shall never happen again. Israel has had too much history.

ISRAEL: A NATION TOO YOUNG TO DIE

JAMES A. MICHENER

Many words have been written about the explosive situation which exists between Jew and Arab in the Middle-East, but very few are as eloquent as James Michener's personal impressions of the drama and meaning of today's struggle in the Holy Land.

I remember when I first became aware of the unnatural tension under which the citizens of Israel have been obliged to live since the establishment of their nation in 1948. I had come to the seaport city of Haifa to do research on a book, and for well over a year, I stayed there, probing the various libraries at my disposal.

Almost every week, and often three or four times a week, my morning paper carried the news that one or another leading Arab politician, and not infrequently a head of state of one of the neighboring Arab countries, had announced his intention of leading an army that would "push the Jews of Israel into the sea," or that would "wipe them off the face of the earth," or perhaps, "strangle them forever." I suppose that the threats occurring during the time I worked in Israel totaled well over a hundred.

They came from more than a half-dozen different countries, some as far away as Algeria and Morocco, whose pre-

James A. Michener. "Israel: A Nation Too Young to Die," *Look* Magazine (August 8, 1967).

occupation with Israel I could not understand. They did not come, so far as I remember, from Lebanon or Jordan, which have common boundaries with Israel.

Especially appalling to me were the five different times when some Arab head of state announced that he was going to blow up the city in which I sat working. I took even those threats without panic, for I have seen a good deal of war and bombing and do not frighten easily, but I must admit that, when the Arab leaders narrowed down their target to the hotel in which I was sitting and when on two occasions they gave a specific timetable for dispatching their rockets, I felt shivers run up my spine.

I lived for more than a year under these constant threats. I neutralized them by saying, "I'm free to leave Israel when I like. I have no personal attachments and no responsibility." But what must have been the accumulated anxiety for the head of a growing family in Haifa, who heard these threats each week, not for one year but for nineteen? What must have been his feelings if he knew that he could not leave the threatened country, that he had a responsibility both to his family and to his nation?

Israel's apprehension was not a paper one. In addition to the threats, there were constant incursions into Israel, constant shootings across the borders, constant intrusions by groups as large as squadrons or small companies. If I went to do some research on the old synagogue at Korazim, I was somewhat taken aback to find that one day later, a pitched battle had been fought there and two Israeli citizens had been killed. If I went on a picnic to the Sea of Galilee, I was a bit shaken when two days later, there was a bombardment of Israeli boats. If I visited the kibbutz at Dan and waded upstream to the cool spring that forms one of the headwaters of the River Jordan, I was frightened to learn that, shortly before, a man had been lost doing that. And when I moved to Jerusalem, to work in the libraries there, I was sorrowful when children told me I must not walk down this alley by the Persian synagogue; gunfire had been coming in from the rooftops only 50 feet away.

And wherever I went, whether to Haifa, or to Korazim, or the Galilee, or Beersheba, there was the constant dinning in my ears of the threat, reiterated week after week, "We are going to destroy you. We are going to push you into the sea." The history of Israel is the history of ordinary people living ordinary lives under the incessant repetition of that threat, backed up by just enough Arab military activity to prove that the threat might be put into action at any moment.

To understand the problem of Israel, the outsider must imagine himself living in Washington, D.C., and reading each morning that neighbors in Baltimore and Alexandria have again threatened to blow Washington off the face of the earth and to push all Washingtonians into the Potomac. The threat, mind you, does not come from across the Atlantic or Pacific. It comes from a few miles away. And to prove the reality of the threat, actual military adventures occur from time to time, taking the lives of random Washingtonians.

What chance would you say there was for the citizens of Washington to go on indefinitely ignoring such behavior? This article is an account of why the citizens of Israel had to react to such a situation.

I must point out at the beginning that I hold no special brief for either the Israelis or Jews in general. I have lived too long among them to retain any starry-eyed visions. They are ordinary people, marred by ordinary weaknesses and bolstered by the courage that ordinary men of all nations and races can at times draw upon. I worked among Muslims for ten years before I ever set foot in Israel, and on at least 50 percent of the characteristics by which men and societies are judged, I like Muslims at least as well as I like the Jews.

Furthermore, I am a professional writer who has worked in many contrasting societies, and I have found none inherently superior to all others. There have been many single aspects of Japan, or Polynesia, or Spain, or India, or Afghanistan that I have preferred, and to me, Israel is merely one more country. It happens to have certain characteristics that elicit enormous respect, but so did each of the Muslim countries in which I worked.

What we are concerned with here is a problem of worldwide significance: How can nations that must live side by side do so with a decent regard one for the other? In trying to reach a solution to this problem, Israel has as many responsibilities as its neighbors. However, this particular inquiry relates primarily to certain adjustments the Arabs must make before any kind of stability can be achieved in a region where stability is much to be desired.

Exactly how vicious were the verbal threats? It will be instructive, I think, to follow the behavior of one Arab country over a short period of time so that the non-Middle Easterner can catch something of the quality of the attacks that were constantly being made. For this purpose, I have chosen Syria, which has a common frontier with Israel and an internal political problem that makes verbal attacks on Israel an attractive form of demagoguery.

For some years, Syria's politics have been unusually volatile. During my stay in the area, there were several revolutions, three complete changes of government, and continued violence. At one time, observers had hoped that Syria's political union with Egypt might produce a substantial and stable bloc of Arab power that would carry with it a sense of responsibility. But that union did not last long, and with its dissolution, Syria plunged into contortions that carried it first in one direction, then another. Consequently, Syrian politicians found that the one thing that united them was a common call for violence against Israel. This is how they spoke:

March 13, 1966, the official newspaper, Al Baath: "It has become evident that our problem will only be solved by an armed struggle to expel the rapacious enemy, and put an end to the Zionist presence."

April 17, 1966, the chief of state of the country, Nureddin Al-Attassi, in a speech at a military parade: "A total popular war of liberation is the only way to liberate Palestine and foil the plan of imperialism and reaction . . . We shall work for the mobilization of all efforts for the needs of the total popular war of liberation."

May 12, 1966, the Syrian commander in chief: "As for the statements of the so-called ministers and officials in Israel that they will punish states which support the commando forces . . . we tell them that we shall wage a liberation war against them as the Party has decided, and fear and alarm will fill every house in Israel."

May 19, 1966, Radio Damascus: "When our revolution declared that the way to liberate Palestine is through a popular war, it knew beforehand that the meaning of this declaration is an open and decisive confrontation with Israel."

May 22, 1966, Chief of State Al-Attassi: "We raise the slogan of the people's liberation war. We want total war with no limits, a war that will destroy the Zionist base."

May 24, 1966, Syrian Defense Minister Hafez Assad: "We say: We shall never call for, nor accept peace . . . We have resolved to drench this land with our blood, to oust you, aggressors, and throw you into the sea for good."

July 16, 1966, Premier Yousef Zouayer: "The popular liberation war which the Palestinian masses, backed by the Arab masses in the whole Arab homeland, have determined to wage, will foil the methods of Israel and those behind it. We say to Israel: Our reply will be harsh and it will pay dearly."

It must be remembered that the above quotations come from a period of relative stability along the Syrian-Israeli frontier. In the succeeding nine months, from September, 1966, through May, 1967, or just before the outbreak of armed hostilities, both the tempo and the inflammability increased. In those weeks when Syria was not threatening to destroy Israel, the heads of other Arab nations were. During my stay in Israel, I believe all the Arab states, excepting Jordan and Lebanon, made specific announcements that they were preparing a war that would drive Israel into the sea.

This constant incendiary barrage came to a climax in May of 1967, when war against Israel had pretty well been agreed upon, and perhaps that accounts for the exaggerated quality of these statements:

May 25, 1967, Cairo radio, in a broadcast to all Arab countries: "The Arab people is firmly resolved to wipe Israel off the map."

May 26, 1967, President Gamal Abdel Nasser of Egypt: "Our basic aim will be to destroy Israel."

May 26, 1967, the leader of the Palestine Liberation Organization, Ahmed Shukairy: "D-day is approaching. The Arabs have waited 19 years for this and will not flinch from the war of liberation."

May 29, 1967, the same Mr. Shukairy: "The struggle has begun at the Gulf of Aqaba and will end at the Bay of Acre."

May 30, 1967, Cairo radio: "Faced by the blockade of the Gulf of Aqaba, Israel has two choices, both of which are drenched with Israel's blood: Either it will be strangled by the Arab military and economic siege or it will be killed by the bullets of the Arab armies surrounding it from the South, from the North and from the East."

June 1, 1967, the commander of the Egyptian Air Force on Egyptian television: "The Egyptian forces spread from Rafah to Sharm el Sheik are ready for the order to begin the struggle to which we have looked forward for so long."

Now, I suppose that a logical man ought to reason: "If the leaders of the Arab states confine their threats to verbalisms, no matter how virulent, the citizens of Israel should adjust to the situation, for obviously the Arabs are using words in a way that need not be taken seriously." Speaking for myself, after my initial weeks of shock, I began to dismiss the blasts against Israel as bombast.

I tried to quiet my inner fears and become adjusted to this incessant barrage of verbal threats, but my ability to live with them did not mean that I was immune to them. Not at all. For whether I liked it or not, I was living under an act of aggression. That it was psychological rather than physical made it the more insidious. I began to find that, although in public I dismissed the threats as evidence of temporary insanity on the part of those who made them, when I was alone, I had to worry about them. Against my will, I found myself concluding, "If Syria and Egypt and Iraq and the others keep on making such threats, they must in the end do something about them. And if Israelis continue to hear these threats week after week, they must in the end accept them as real, and they, too, will have to act upon them."

In this way, not only were the airwaves polluted, not only was all intercourse between nations contaminated and all chance of peaceful coexistence frustrated, but the psychological processes of both those who made the threats and those who received them were slowly and painfully corroded until both Arab and Jew knew that war was inevitable. On one visit to Jordan, which was one of the least psychotic areas, I talked with 16 young Arabs and all said they longed for the day when they could march with the Arab armies into Israel and wipe it off the face of the earth. In Egypt, I found attitudes the same. And what was most regrettable, in Israel, where I knew thousands of persons who would speak frankly, a dull kind of resignation possessed them: "I suppose that one of these days we shall have to defend ourselves again."

It is because of the danger that thrives on verbal threats that English common law evolved the concept of assault and battery. Not many laymen appreciate that, in law, the threat to do bodily damage is roughly the same as physically doing it. But society has learned that the continued psychological damage to the threathened victim is often graver than an actual punch in the nose might have been. The threat involves uncertainty and accumulating fear, whereas the physical release of an actual blow is over and done with in an instant. Thus, in strict legality, if I hold a gun and threaten, "I am going to shoot you," that is an assault. If I actually do the shooting, it is a battery. The important thing, however, is that the law holds the two things roughly equal, and a private citizen may be as quickly thrown in jail for one as for the other.

When assault is resorted to by nations, it is a violation of the United Nations Charter, Article 2, Principle number 4. Yet for 19 years, Israel lived under constant assaults.

In spite of my knowledge that a verbal assault is sometimes more destructive than a physical battery, in spite of my recognition of Arab behavior as aggression, and in spite of my experience with history that proves one aggression breeds another, I still clung to my hope that as long as the Syrians and the Egyptians confined themselves to wordy abuse, Israel could learn to live with it as one of the peculiarities of Arab politics. I even began to understand why nations as far away as Morocco, Algeria, and Pakistan wanted to participate in the verbal campaign, for in this way, they kept their franchise as Muslim states. I was pleased to see that more mature Muslim sovereignties like Turkey, Iran, and even Arab Tunisia wanted no part of this folly. Again and again, I told my Israeli friends and others who asked me, "As long as the Arabs confine themselves to verbal threats alone, no great damage will be done."

Unfortunately, the surrounding countries did not confine themselves to verbalisms. They also engaged in open acts of invasion, sabotage, terrorism, and military action. I myself witnessed the aftermaths of three such actions.

One day in 1963, I visited the ancient black-basalt synagogue at Korazim because I wanted to see how Jews had worshiped in the time of Christ. It is believed that Jesus once lectured there, and I found ruins not often visited by tourists. It was a remote area, peaceful, indifferent, as old almost as the hills. But on the next day, Syrian armed units invaded this rural scene and killed two civilians. Hotheads in Syria boasted that this was part of a planned program of harassment that would continue until all Jews were driven into the sea.

Again in 1963, I visited the Kibbutz Ein Gev for one of its famous fish dinners and a lazy afternoon of watching boats drifting across the Sea of Galilee. I also climbed up into the hills in back of Ein Gev to see the incredible kibbutz perched on the last half inch of Israeli soil. As I sat in the dining room, whose windows were shielded by a massive concrete bunker, a young Israeli girl explained, "We have to have the wall to keep out the Syrian bullets, for they shoot at us whenever we sit down to eat." Two days after my visit, a Syrian gun emplacement in the hills lobbed shells into the lake, sank a fishing boat and injured five fishermen. Once more, Syria publicly announced that this was part of a continuing campaign.

My most moving experience came when I visited the beautiful Catholic monastery marking the supposed site of Christ's Sermon on the Mount. It rests on the hills west of Capernaum, where Jesus sometimes argued with scholars, and while I was staying there, I learned that shortly before, in Israeli fields to the east, a Syrian patrol had planted land mines and one had exploded, killing Israeli farmers.

I could go on through the years 1964, 1965, 1966, and 1967, citing incident after incident in which acts of actual warfare were perpetrated in this region. From the high hills that Syria occupied to the east, gun positions pumped in random shots at workers on the Israeli farms. From protected emplacements along the shore of the Sea of Galilee, Syrian guns fired point-blank at Israeli fishermen. And night after night, marauding parties crept over the border to mine, to murder and destroy.

Now, no man in his right mind would claim that Israel in the meantime was sitting idly by in childish innocence, or that it accepted these invasions of its sovereignty without striking back. In self-respect, there had to be retaliations, and there were. These war-like Arab acts, backing up verbal threats, would have been suicidal for the Israeli Government to ignore. Arab leaders now began massing enormous armies with much first-rate equipment, and these gave every evidence of being able to crush Israel. What was most provocative of all, the leaders of this might openly announced that they planned to launch a full-scale war. If ever a nation was forewarned by word and act and specific promise of annihilation, it was Israel.

What were the odds against Israel? A quick glance at the figures—46 million in the surrounding Arab countries, 97 million in all, as against 2.6 million Israelis—might lead one to believe that the Arab states would have little trouble in overwhelming Israel, except that twice before, in 1948 and 1956, they had tried to do so and failed. Arab leaders grew adept in explaining away the somber fact that, twice, a handful of Jews had resisted efforts to throw them into the sea. "In 1948," explained the leaders, "we were betrayed by Great Britain, and in 1956, it was the French and English armies that defeated us through their invasion of the Suez." By June, 1967, a persuasive legend had grown up, largely masking the truth that the Arab states had ever tested arms with the Israelis, and completely ignoring that in each war, the Israelis had been victorious. In a magic flood of words, history was repealed.

The Arab leaders created an enticing world of fantasy; one demagogue lived on the pronouncements of the other, and in time, all came to believe that facts were other than they had been. When the Arab armies were able to import huge supplies of modern weapons from their East European supporters, they really believed that their peasant levies, with little stake in their society to fight for, would stand up against Israelis who had good homes, better universities, and a deep moral commitment to their nation.

I have had two opportunities to witness the impact of

this fantasy world upon rational Arabs. In one of my books, I described in some detail the manner in which, in 1948, Jewish youths captured the north Israel city of Safad against overwhelming numbers of Arab soldiers. At no point in my description did I deride the Arabs or cast aspersions upon them. Some dozen correspondents in the different Arab nations commented upon this favorably when they wrote to me complaining about the passage. What they objected to were the facts I presented. Some claimed that the Jews must have numbered 20 or 30 times their known strength. Others argued that Arab units that we know to have been in the city were not really there. Several explained that the loss was due to British perfidy in turning over to the Jews the best military sites, whereas the truth was just the opposite. And all expressed the opinion that I had been tricked by a legend that had not really happened. I had the strange feeling that my correspondents trusted that, one morning they would waken to find that Safad had never really been lost at all, that it was still in Arab hands, and that maps and stories to the contrary had been mere propaganda.

Of course, in the preceding paragraph, I am generalizing from a dozen letters, none of whose authors did I see personally, and it may be that I am reading into their letters a greater evidence of fantasy than the writers showed. About my second experience, I cannot make such an error, for it I witnessed in person.

In the summer of 1964, I was vacationing in the lovely city of Alexandria, made famous by the writers of antiquity and by Charles Kingsley and Lawrence Durrell, and one day at sunset, as I was strolling along that unequaled boulevard that runs beside the Mediterranean, I came to a park, where in the evenings, a concert of folk music was offered. Now, I am very partial to this form of entertainment, for one learns much from uncontaminated folk songs. So I bought a ticket for the performance.

At the concert, I found a large number of Egyptian families with their children. It was a splendid night, filled with stars and coolness, and we sat back to watch a first-class performance of folk song and dance. The choruses were strong, the dancers agile, and the evening compared with others I had enjoyed in Kyoto, Djakarta, Manila, and Mexico City.

A rather large cast performed, and this made me wonder where the money to pay them came from, for the audience was not unusually big and the prices we had paid were only nominal. I shrugged my shoulders and concluded that this was someone else's problem, but when the regular performance had ended, without a false note that I could detect, the bugles started blowing, excitement gripped the children in the audience, and the curtains parted to show a scene in the year A.D. 2000. In a park much like the one in which we were sitting, a group of children played about the statue of an Egyptian soldier while an old man watched. One of the children asked who the statue was, and by means of a dance, the old fellow explained. Years dropped from his shoulders. His cane became a gun. His ragged clothes fell away to reveal a military uniform, and as more bugles blew, ghosts of his former companions in arms appeared onstage, and in wonderfully choreographed pantomime, the Egyptian Army demonstrated how it had won the great war of 1956.

The scene was at Suez, where a handful of heroic Egyptians held off and finally defeated not an Israeli army but invaders storming ashore from French and English battleships. For each Egyptian soldier, scores of Frenchmen and Englishmen rushed onstage, only to be overwhelmed by sheer courage. In the end, the invaders had to retreat, whereupon the Egyptian defenders fell into a tableau of victory as fine as any I had ever seen. The great powers had been driven off, and Egyptian honor was once more secure.

I looked about me at the audience, and it was apparent that the adults, many of whom must have participated in the events thus portrayed, had begun to accept this version as history. Their eyes glowed, and a real patriotism suffused their faces. As we left the park, I saw one young boy of nine or ten lunging out with an imaginary bayonet to hold off imaginary Frenchmen and Englishmen. When I made inquiries about the performance, I found that it was paid for by the government and was repeated throughout the year.

The whole thing was fantasy, of course, and certainly no worse than similar versions of English history offered in London or French history in Paris. I am sure that parallel perversions could be found in American folklore, and I doubt that much harm is done to children by this patriotic nonsense. But in the case of Egypt and the other Arab lands, there was an additional danger because adults, too, were accepting such fables: college professors, university students, newspaper editors, businessmen believed that Egypt had won a great victory in 1956. I could find no evidence that anyone in public life was willing to admit that, in Egypt's military adventure against a handful of Jews, the latter had easily won.

All nations engage in fantasy, but few indulge themselves with so virulent a dream as the twofold Arab dream that Israel does not exist and that the Jews who presently occupy the land of Israel can easily be pushed into the Mediterranean—whenever the Arabs finally decide to do so.

Sometime in the spring of 1967, the Arab leaders decided that the time was ripe. Under incessant pressure of Ahmed Shukairy, leader of the Palestine Liberation Organization, who stood to win himself the satrapy of Palestine if he could goad Egypt, Syria, Iraq, Lebanon, Jordan, and Saudi Arabia into declaring war on Israel, and with the full connivance of Gamal Abdel Nasser, who stood to win himself an emperorship if the war was successful, the Arab nations reached an understanding. These men who had lived so long on fantasy now conceived the supreme fantasy that they could quickly destroy the nation that had twice defeated them and had, in the interim, grown stronger socially, psychologically, and morally, even though its airplanes and tanks had not kept pace in numbers with those of the Arabs.

On May 16, 1967, President Nasser initiated the two final moves. On that day, he elbowed the United Nations Emergency Force out of its peacekeeping positions along the Egyptian-Israeli border in the Sinai Peninsula and forced it ignominiously to retire from the area, thus depriving Israel of the one slim assurance it had that a surprise attack would not be launched from the desert. The fire engine that was supposed to protect the community scuttled out of town at the first smell of smoke. In its place, President Nasser moved up his own divisions, and the stage was set for war.

On May 22, 1967, he made his second crucial move. With the retreat of the United Nations troops, he found himself in sole control of Sharm el Sheik, the fortress commanding the strait leading into the Gulf of Aqaba. It was a simple matter for him to announce that, henceforth, the Gulf would be closed to Israeli ships and even to ships of other nations carrying strategic materials bound for Israel. None would be permitted to enter and none to leave. This was a hostile act, and had to be construed as a declaration of war. That President Nasser was aware of the gravity of his act, he took no pains to hide: "Sharm el Sheik and the blockade mean real confrontation with Israel. Taking such a step means that we should be ready to enter full-scale war with Israel. It is not an isolated operation."

The Gulf has been recognized as an international waterway because four sovereign nations line its coasts: on the east, Saudi Arabia; on the west, Egypt; on the north, Israel; and on the northeast, Jordan. But it is more important economically to Israel than to any of the other three since Elath is a major port for handling oil and other heavy cargoes. If the Gulf of Aqaba were to be closed to all shipping, whether to Jordon or Israel, the blockade would damage Jordan, but it would prostrate Israel. However, ships intended for Jordan were allowed to pass, and during the exercise of the blockade, several did proceed unmolested to Jordan. This underlined the fact that the blockade was meant to be an act of war, and lest any misunderstand the intention, President Nasser proclaimed on May 26:

> "The Arab people want to fight . . .
>
> "We have been waiting for the suitable day when we shall be completely ready, since, if we enter a battle with Israel, we should be confident of victory and should take strong measures. We do not speak idly.
>
> "We have lately felt that our strength is sufficient, and that if we enter the battle with Israel, we shall, with God's help, be victorious. Therefore, we have now decided that I take real steps.
>
> "The battle will be a full-scale one, and our basic aim will be to destroy Israel."

Obviously, the major maritime nations of the world, having anticipated that such a blockade might one day be attempted, in which case their ships would be powerless to enter the narrow strait, had long been on record regarding two points: (1) the Gulf of Aqaba was an international waterway, and (2) as such, it must be kept open for all nations to use equally without let or hindrance.

By flouting international law and blockading the Gulf of Aqaba to Israeli shipping, President Nasser had effectively and somewhat cleverly cut Israel's lifeline to the south. If the blockade were allowed to continue unchallenged, Israel would experience what its Arab neighbors had been threatening for so long—its strangulation. This was war, but still only an indirect version, in the economic field. One could reasonably hope that from it, President Nasser might back away, but such hopes were dashed on May 28, when he announced over the radio: "We intend to open a general assault against Israel. This will be total war. Our basic aim is the destruction of Israel."

As the Arabs prepared for what they assured themselves

was to be the final conquest of Israel, their morale was at high pitch. And because of what they had been told so continuously over the previous eight years regarding their victory over the British and French in 1956, they believed in all honesty that this time they were going to crush Israel, and fairly easily.

President Nasser encouraged this belief by his belligerent speeches. From Syria, Chief of State Al-Attassi thundered that his army was impatient to begin marching.

The foot soldiers, the aviators, the tank commanders, and even the generals prepared to launch what they were convinced would be an easy, victorious sortie. In the fantasy world in which they had lived for so long and to which they had contributed, words took the place of accomplishment, wishes took the place of military discipline, and inflated dreams of revenge superseded facts.

If the Arabs with their verbal assaults had made life difficult for Israel, they had perpetrated a worse crime against themselves; for they had come to believe their own inflated nonsense.

At the hour of attack, the Voice of the Arabs radio station in Cairo issued this stirring call to its soldiers. It is the usual heartening battle cry that all nations use at a time of crisis and in general purpose is not much different from what Englishmen or Russians or Americans would shout to their soldiers; but in the cry for avenging 1948, one hears a unique and ominous overtone:

> "Destroy, ruin, liberate. Woe to Israel, your hour has arrived. The Arab nation is on its way to render its account. O Israel, this is your end.
>
> "Every Arab must take revenge for 1948, must cross the Armistice lines from all directions and head for Tel Aviv. We shall drive out of existence the shame of Zionism. Rescue the looted Palestine. Hit everywhere till the end.

> "There is no room for Israel in Palestine. This is your responsibility, O Arab soldiers! Israel, taste death!"

It required less than 72 hours in June to deflate this bombast.

What can be done to awaken the Arab masses to the reality that Israel stands where it does and will presumably remain there for some centuries? In the aftermath of 1948, the rest of the world permitted and perhaps encouraged the Arabs to follow a policy of blinding refusing to admit that Israel existed. The armistice commissions, which should have worked out regional policies, were not permitted to operate effectively. Decisions upon which peace depended could not be made because the Arabs refused to acknowledge that history had produced an old-new nation that would prove most viable—that was too young to die. The normal intercourse between nations, such as is conducted between Russia and Germany, which were certainly as bitter enemies as Egypt and Israel, was forbidden, and the region fumbled its way to the war of 1956.

When Israel won handily, the refusal to admit realities persisted, and the same errors were allowed to continue. International commissions did not function, and normal intercourse between nations did not mature, even though the Arab portion of the region and the Israeli form a marvelous, interlocking whole—a unit whose various segments could well profit from economic, medical, educational, developmental, and planning cooperation. The blindness and the arrogant folly that produced this stalemate also produced the speeches cited in this article. And they in turn produced the hysteria that led to a third war in less than 20 years.

If the world, in 1948, had insisted that the nations of this area sit down in honest consultation, 1956 might have been avoided. If the world, following the disaster of 1956, had insisted that the Arab nations at least awaken to the existence of Israel, the tremendous folly of 1967 could have been avoided. Now, the world has a third chance, and if some right decisions are made in the months ahead, the even greater tragedy of 1977 may be avoided. What is necessary is a reasonable revision of boundary lines; a sensible settlement of the Palestinian refugee problem; a cessation of verbal assault and physical battery; and a union of talents and interests, of resources and abilities, so that the region can move forward to a creative society in which all members live infinitely better than anyone there now does.

Am I hopeful that the world will now sensibly tackle its problems, when it refused to do so in the aftermath of 1948 and 1956? I am not. President Gamal Abdel Nasser pulled out of the hat one of the cleverest tricks of his career when, in the first hours of defeat, he invented the enticing theory that once again it was not Israelis who were crushing his armed might from every direction but English and Americans, and within a few days it was adopted as official dogma. In 1970, when I revisit the lovely waterfront of Alexandria, I expect to see a tableau explaining how, in a moment of travail in the spring of 1967, the Egyptians and their Arab allies stood bravely against the combined air might of Great Britain and the United States and repulsed it. That Israel was involved will not be mentioned.

At the moment when Egyptian armies were suffering the worst defeats, Egypt's undefeated radio was broadcasting the following careful analysis of the situation:

> "The United States is the enemy. Its fighters and bombers gathered in large groups to provide for Israel an air umbrella that prevents the Arabs from bombing Israel's towns and villages, while it is moving fast all along the occupied frontiers of the Arabs. The United States, therefore, is the Aggressor.
>
> "The United States saw Israel about to collapse under the blow of death. The Chicago gangs moved; the state of gangsterism and bloodshed moved; it moved in order

to protect its aggressive base in the Middle East. How vile and treacherous the United States has been in its collusion with the Zionists! It refrained from coming out openly to fight us. It refrained from facing the Arabs with an open and daring hostility. No, Arabs. The United States is too vile and too base to have the ethics of cavaliers. The United States threw, from all its airports and aircraft carriers in the Mediterranean, huge and continuous massings of its fighters and bombers in order to provide that air umbrella that protected Israel from the revenge of the Arabs, from the massings of the Arabs, and from the victory of the Arabs.

"The battle is continuing, United States . . . It is going on until you become, as Britain became after the 1956 collusion, a third-rate state. Here we shall bury the American international gangsterism. Here, Arabs, dig graves everywhere; dig them for every U.S. existence; dig them. Arabs. Dig all the homeland a grave for U.S. existence. Dig it, Arabs. Dig it, Arabs. Dig it, Arabs.

"The curse of all the Arabs, from the ocean to the gulf and from every corner of the globe, is on you, America, and on your lackey, Israel; together with the curse of all free peoples, the curse of free men everywhere."

On the night when the defeat of the Arab armies was known to the world as one of the most crushing in history, I discussed matters on an all-night radio show with Dr. M. T. Mehdi, secretary-general of the Action Committee on American-Arab Relations, and he made these points: "Nothing has changed. Israel is worse than Nazi Germany, and the Arabs will have to drive her from the region. The war will continue precisely as it has been going for the past 19 years. And what the Americans and the English took away from the Arabs by their intervention, the Arabs will recover at the conference table. Peace talks, of course, will have to be conducted through third parties at the United Nations, because no Arab leader will ever agree to sit down and talk with an outlaw nation like Israel. You'll see. The United Nations will force Israel back to her 1948 boundaries, after which all Arab nations will unite in a war to exterminate her, because this is going to be just like the Crusades. For two hundred years, the Arabs will continue their fight, and in the end, they'll do exactly what they've said. Push Israel into the sea."

Nasser will probably gain more from the Arab world in defeat than he would have gained in victory. The war made him a tragic hero around whom the emotional Arabs can rally. Soon, his new crop of generals will be making the old speeches of 1948, 1956, and 1967. His people will believe them, for fantasy is impossible to eradicate if one's whole society is structured on the perpetuation of the Arabian Nights.

Yet we must dispel that fantasy. To do so is the job to which we are all committed—unless we are content to watch this pathetic farce of Arab self-delusion repeated in 1977, 1988 and 1999.

O JERUSALEM

MAX LERNER

The wailing wall of Jerusalem may well be the focal point not only of the state of Israel but of the Jewish religion as well. It is the last standing section of the Second Temple of King Solomon, and generation upon generation of Jews have gone to worship there. From the 1948 War of Independence until the Six-Day War of 1967, it lay in Arab hands.

Max Lerner discusses Jewish "rights" to the wall and describes the joy felt by Israelis at possessing it once again.

It is not the war I am writing about, nor even the ceasefire and the peace. It is the pictures and newspaper stories of the line of Israeli soldiers in battle dress, with prayerbooks in their hands, standing in prayer at the Wailing Wall in Old Jerusalem after they had captured that portion of the city from the Jordanian army. If one need a single emblem of what was in the minds and hearts of the Israelis in the fantastic Four Days War of June, 1967, this is the emblem—this joyful welling of the heart, beyond ordinary tears or rejoicing, at being able once more to stand at a corner of the ruins of King Solomon's Temple, and after two thousand years, to be again in possession of it.

Whether the Israelis, as Jews, have been there before or are only intruders in the Arab dust is more than an idle academic question. It goes to the heart of the whole current global debate about the state of Israel and the Arab states. It is a case where a judgment about history becomes a judgment about contemporary policy.

Max Lerner. "O Jerusalem," *The New York Post* (June 12, 1967).

If indeed the modern Jews settled in Palestine only to grab up some land, belonging historically to the Arabs, or as outposts of a British or American imperialist power drive, then one must identify with the Arab anger at being displaced by superior science and technology.

But if the deep roots of the Jews as a historical community were indeed in Judea, if they were dispersed over the world by superior power, if one of the dreams that kept them alive in the Diaspora was the dream that some of them would some day return, then their settlement of the land was a quest for identity as a people, as well as a respite from their exile. In that case, all the shifting boundary lines since the British mandate, with or without UN resolutions and Great Power guarantees, become temporarily expressions of modern power politics to be viewed against the backdrop of the continuity of five thousand years of history.

Life contains the ache of loss and the ache of triumph. The Jews as a historical community have had both. The loss was there, with the destruction of the Temple and the laying waste of the city. ("If I forget thee, O Jerusalem . . .") And now the triumph is there too, so that it should not be too hard, even for non-Israelis, to understand the poignancy behind General Moshe Dayan's comment as he stood by the Wailing Wall: "We have returned to the holiest of our holy places, never to depart from it again."

Never to depart? By what right? Not only the right of victory, after having been encircled and threatened with total extirpation, but—far beyond that—the right of reclaiming an ancient tradition, religious and civil alike, and reuniting the broken parts of a great historic city so that it will have an organic oneness.

But surely, the Christian and Moslem religions have their shrines in Jerusalem too. History weaves a complex tapestry, and three great religions have arisen out of the religion-creating soil of a tiny slice of the Middle East. For a brief spell, since 1949, the Jordanians alone were trustees of the holy places of all three faiths. It is an understatement to say that the Israelis can be counted on, with greater fidelity, to preserve all three.

It is amazing to note how clarifying victory is in dispelling doubts and confusions. Many people who were certain that the little band of Israelis was doomed, and rightly doomed perhaps, at the hands of the encircling planes and armor of the Arabs, now perceive all kinds of reasons to explain the Israeli victory. Mostly the reasons run in terms of the efficiency and modernity of the Israeli army. But this can be overdone. Efficiency, yes, and modernity, yes, especially as against the feudal structure of Arab society. But efficiency and modernity in the service of what?

The answer is, I think, in the service of historic continuity and humanist values and the life of the mind. If we make a cult simply of efficiency and modernity, then what difference was there between the Israeli tanks cutting through the Sinai desert and the desert tactics of Rommel in World War II? Or between the Israeli blitz and the Nazi blitz? It is not technics alone that count, but technics in the service of humanism.

If one wishes a single stripped-down reason for the Israeli victory, it lies in those pictures of the Israeli soldiers at the Wailing Wall and the historic continuity they suggest. All throughout the centuries the Jews have been the People of the Book, keeping alive the tradition and the functioning of the life of the mind. That is what they have to build on in the post-war days ahead, and that is what they have to contribute to a community of coexistence with the Arabs.

ISRAEL: THE NEXT TWENTY YEARS

J. ROBERT MOSKIN

Although Israel is confidently approaching its twenty-first year as a state, the young nation does have a great many difficulties, both internal and external, that it will have to solve if it is, indeed, to reach middle age and beyond. Mr. Moskin, foreign editor of Look *Magazine, enumerates the most pressing problems facing Israel and reflects upon the possible solutions to them.*

It will be a miracle if Israel survives another 20 years. But then, it has been a miracle that it survived its first 20. These have been years of siege and strain. The siege goes on; the strains grow more taut. There are no guarantees for the future.

One who returns to Israel since the Six Day War last June senses a new tone of exaltation, a new self-assurance. Last spring, these people feared extermination—the word was bitterly familiar—then they struck back and laid waste their enemies. Now, they feel, they have to thank no one; they saved themselves. Many who had not been at all religious now see the presence of God on their side. The Old Testament spirit seems to them to live again.

If the Israelis feel cocky and Chosen, they are also tense. In Jerusalem, young soldiers walk with their girls along Jaffa Road in the evening, a submachine gun slung under one arm. Everyone talks endlessly of the war, the Arabs, the Russians.

J. Robert Moskin. "Israel: The Next Twenty Years," *Look* Magazine (April 30, 1968).

They point to the bullet scars on their apartment buildings. And some grieve.

One night recently, I took a taxi from Tel Aviv up to Jerusalem. I was returning from a long day's journey in military convoy across the Sinai desert to the ghost-quiet Suez Canal. It was after midnight, and the young stocky driver stopped, got out, and from the trunk took a pistol and tucked it in his belt. Then he chose the shorter road, which was the original route to Jerusalem before the fighting in 1948 and for 19 years ran through Jordanian territory. (Israelis don't know whether to call it the "new road" or the "old road." Since June, a lot of old things suddenly are new.) And in the darkness, climbing through the moonlit Judean hills, we talked. He is a Sabra—born in Palestine. His father and older brother were killed by the Arabs in the 1948 war. And now he is a paratrooper, already a veteran of three wars. He expects to have to fight again.

"I love this country," he said. "It is more mine than the Arabs'. I am used to war; I'm not afraid. I know we can't trust anyone—especially not the Arabs. I know about Jaffa in 1938 and Hebron in 1936 and 1929, when they killed their Jewish neighbors in their beds. We must be strong and not bow our heads. That's the most important thing. This war showed people that I was right. We should have finished it. If we had gone to Cairo and Damascus, they would not be talking. They would be quiet. It would be finished!"

This young civilian paratrooper is more militant than most Israelis—and much more outspoken. But as he says, the war is not finished. The Israelis believe the Arab has not gotten it through his head that Israel intends to survive. They want their borders secured against attack (as much as borders can be). They would like to trade with their Arab neighbors, develop resources and tourism jointly, and work out together problems of water and communications and roads—and maybe someday a common market, even a common defense.

Prime Minister Levi Eshkol pounded his knee as he said to me, "We would like to have peace—not only a coerced thing but we would like to reach an understanding with our neighbors . . . I am talking as a prime minister to a president (Nasser). We are ready to meet everywhere and every day."

There is little reason for optimism. Arab pride is deeply cut. The Arab world's internal problems are so mountainous that its leaders can only scream about the enemy outside. In that sense, too, the young paratrooper is right. The Israelis would be foolish not to stay strong.

And they are not foolish. They face an array of tough problems. Even if they are often too rigid and assertive to agree on solutions, they see the issues clearly. Today in Israel is a time of reexamination. To judge Israel's prospects and what this society will be like in the future, one must examine with candor its six most urgent problems.

1. THE ARABS OUTSIDE. If there could be peace, Arabs and Israelis together could make the Middle East a garden. But there is no peace; the Middle East is a mess.

Israeli military service has been lengthened to two and a half years, and the defense budget drains the economy. Arab armies are being resupplied by the Russians. Attacks on Israel continue, by terrorists with Russian and Communist Chinese Arms, and goad Israeli reactions such as occurred recently across the Jordan River from Jericho. And most important, the June war has hardened the Arabs' belligerency with a coating of sullen humiliation. Without a change in attitude, even a peace treaty would be a scrap of paper.

The land the 2.6 million Israelis occupy, the Arabs believe is theirs. They still find Israel's very existence unbearable. Some fear that Israel really wants to rule from the Nile to the Euphrates. Says Israel's Foreign Minister Abba Eban, "From each war, they derive a new nostalgia, not a new wisdom."

Surprisingly, the Israelis feel little hatred for the Arabs

who threaten them. Partly, this comes from self-confidence; one Israeli says, "Anything they can do, we can do better. Why should we hate?" Partly, it comes from having lived with the Arabs. Says Palestine-born Defense Minister Moshe Dayan:

"I was beaten by them and had stones thrown at me a few times when I was a boy. I was fighting them for 40 years, but I never remember once that I was not offered a meal in an Arab village. I was brought up among them, and I saw the Arab farmer starting his day at four in the morning. I almost envied them their quiet way of life. I don't hate the Arabs. We are living here in a very poor part of the world. You have to work hard here. The Arabs who live here are not the Arabs of Hollywood. They work very hard. Try making your living here without UJA and with so little rain."

But Dayan adds, "Of course, they hate us. They didn't ask us to come to Nablus. If they could, they would have preferred to be in Tel Aviv . . . I (now) have more contact with the Jews in Miami than with the Arabs just across the border."

The Israelis feel the future is up to Egypt's President Nasser. They did not even object when the United States agreed to sell tanks and assorted military hardware to Jordan again in February—better American tanks than Russian, said Dayan. Syria, the Israelis regard as a dangerous "nut house."

Most Israeli leaders predict a period of rearming that could lead to another war. They want to shorten their borders, strengthen the corridor leading to Jerusalem, and prevent a new Syrian threat from the Golan Heights. "The security border line of Israel must be the Jordan," Eshkol told me, adding, "The part of Jerusalem (taken by Israel in the fighting) is a fait accompli." And everyone insists not only on the right of passage through the Strait of Tiran and the Suez Canal but also that the Sinai desert must never again be a staging area for Egyptian armor. Next time, the generals say, they will make sure they bring the downfall of the Arab regimes that strike them.

Foreign Minister Eban says, "If they recognize there are no alternatives—either the present situation or peace—they will choose peace. The present situation is abnormal, but I wouldn't say it is impossible to maintain. The ball is in their court."

In Washington, U.S. officials show most concern about the fate of Jerusalem. For three reasons: Israel is adamant about keeping Arab East Jerusalem. Israel's seizure of the half-city hurts Jordan, which we seem continually trying to make a client state. And King Faisal of Saudi Arabia, where American business has a huge investment, last month started war-whooping for a holy war to get back the Muslim holy places—presumably with U.S. supplied arms.

Israelis have no intention of giving up East Jerusalem. As swiftly as possible last June, Jerusalem's energetic Mayor Teddy Kollek tore down the walls and barbed wire dividing the two halves of the city and pronounced it one. But the Israelis are actively concerned, too, about the Christian and Muslim holy sites, and Dr. Yaacov Herzog, the Dublin-born director general of the Prime Minister's office, has had several meetings with Vatican officials. In the war, the Israelis made special efforts, at the cost of some young Jewish lives, to avoid damaging the holy places, and now they anticipate that the holy places will be given special diplomatic status, with immunity from Israeli police, such as embassies have.

In the decades ahead, much will depend on whether the younger Israeli-born Sabras can find better ways to get along with their hostile neighbors than the old-guard militant Zionists, who have spent years fighting Arabs. In the bleak Jordanian hills beyond Jerusalem on the Hebron road, a group of young people are rebuilding a kibbutz, Kfar Etzion, where the Arab Legion massacred 240 Jewish inhabitants on May 13, 1948, as the nation was born. Only a few fig trees remain from the original kibbutz; the hilltop has been a Jordanian army camp. Now, the sons of those who were killed are returning. They are planting trees and raising sheep and turkeys and flowers. "I believed. I had faith," says one. "I don't feel any hostility against the Arabs. They should only leave us in peace, and we can forget a lot. We have to find a way to live in peace and stop this bloodshed."

In the long run, the Israelis foresee peace. They must. It is too agonizing to see ahead only unending siege and tension and death. Dayan doesn't think Jordan can wait 20 years and says of the Arabs, "They have no alternative." But Major General Itzhak Rabin, last June's chief of staff and now Israel's ambassador to the United States, warns, "It doesn't look to me as though we are going to achieve it in the next few years." And a Foreign Ministry expert says, "Either we will have a peaceful situation in a year's time, or not for 20-25 years." Estimates vary, but maybe in another 20 years, most Israelis say hopefully, they and the Arabs can learn to live peacefully.

2. The Russians' Coming. The Israelis have degraded the Arab armies and no longer fear them. What worries them today is how far the Russians are coming.

Since the Six Day War, the Soviets have resupplied Egypt with 400 jets and 800 tanks, restoring 80 percent of its might, and sent 3,000 advisers, the Israelis say, to retrain its army. The Soviets are entrenched in Damascus. And they have moved an estimated 40 warships into the Mediterranean to counter the American Sixth Fleet. In Washington, officials are disturbed. Says Assistant Secretary of State Lucius Battle, "Peace and stability in the area are essential to us."

Nasser could not make war again without Soviet help, and Israel's new chief of staff, Major General Haim Bar-Lev, says, "What the Russians do in Egypt encourages the Arabs to think they have someone to rely on." But, asks one highly placed Israeli, "When you hug a bear, who hugs whom?"

No one in Jerusalem or Washington can say for sure exactly what are the Soviets' intentions. They certainly want to strengthen Arabs against Western-oriented Israel and the "radical" Arab regimes against the "moderates." Some experts warn they want to dominate Arab oil, which is vital to

Western Europe and counts for a billion dollars in our own balance of payments. But most of all, they want to extend their influence in a crucial, unsettled area. Says a Foreign Ministry official in Jerusalem, "The Russians will go just as far as the United States will let them."

The United States is trying to play it cool, and, busy chasing victory in Vietnam, would settle for a stalemate in the Middle East. Eventually, State Department officials hope Soviet expansionism will clash with Arab nationalism. We want to keep a hand in the factionalized and strife-ridden Arab world, and, says one U.S. diplomat, "We don't want to be isolated with Israel against the Soviet Union and all the Arabs." The Israelis now understand and accept this. "We learned in May and June the great powers canceled each other. We were left alone. Nobody helped us, but nobody interfered with us," says Eban. And Dayan adds, "The United States doesn't want to rely only on the Jews. They'd be crazy."

But General Bar-Lev says, "What is the psychological effect on the Arab world if it sees the Russians are pushing more strength into the area while the United States hasn't done anything at all so far? I think the United States could stop the Russians in continuing to rearm the Arabs simply by proving to them it doesn't pay, that it's only a question of waste of money and waste of lives."

Washington officials want to avoid a confrontation in the Middle East and think the Soviets do too. The Israelis are satisfied if we neutralize the Russians; they will take care of the Arabs. This year, we will supply the Israelis with 48 Skyhawk jet fighters. Says Eshkol, "We don't want your boys. We need tools."

But underneath, the Israelis are nervous about us. They realize our relationship to Israel is based on history, emotion, and a Christian guilty conscience more than on any hard-nosed geopolitical vital interest. They recognize that we want to play footsie with some oil-rich Arabs. They fear we won't stand up strongly enough to the Russians, and they charge that we made a mess in Yemen, where both the Soviet Union and China are involved, and are letting the Russians get a foothold in the Persian Gulf. Their nervousness shows when top officials ask me confidentially whether the U.S. might make a secret deal with the Russians: You help us get out of Vietnam, and we will not oppose you too much in the Middle East. Israelis worry about that.

And who can blame them for being nervous? Our Middle East policy is fuzzy—beyond the platitude that we want peace. And with Britain impotent, France unfriendly, and Russia having switched sides, the Israelis wonder where else, besides the United States, they can turn in the crunch.

Last January, when Prime Minister Eshkol was President Johnson's ranch guest in Texas, the United States promised to increase military support to Israel if the Soviets build up Arab military might beyond some undefined, or at least unpublicized, limit. So, the ladder of escalation is there—in Soviet hands. Whether they climb, it could determine whether Israel is to be permanent or temporary.

3. ECONOMIC PROSPECTS. In 1948, an Israeli pound was worth $4. Today, it is worth 29 cents. Despite remarkable economic progress, Israel, crippled by the costs of defense and immigration, has continually spent more than it earns. It now spends for arms 20 times what it did in 1950. Says Finance Minister Pinhas Sapir, "To save your life, to save Israel, you have to buy Phantoms (U.S. jets)." Without peace, Israel must sustain a warrior state that is expensive in money and manpower. American economist Isador Lubin, consultant on Jewish Appeal expenditures in Israel, says, "They are going to have to tighten their belts and increase their productivity."

To try to straighten out the nation's balance of payments, the government in 1965 created a recession, the *Metun*, to cut domestic consumption. The *Metun* froze wages and prices, squashed the immigrant-inspired building boom, and began to stimulate exports. It also threw out of work many less-skilled, newer immigrants. Says Labor Minister Yigal Allon, "I hope that by this spring there will be full employment again."

Israel has no hydroelectric power, few natural resources, and no cheap labor, so it is trying to exploit the plentiful minerals in the Dead Sea, build an oil pipeline from the Red Sea to the Mediterranean, and start a chemical-and-fertilizer industry. Since last June, its tourism potential has increased significantly. But agriculture, tourism, and the Dead Sea cannot do the job.

Israeli economists assert that exports, which are expected to total $1.1 billion this year, must triple in the next 20 years. Salvation is supposed to come from "science-based industry," using the country's best natural resource: the brains and skills of its European-originated Jews. Planners envision development in electronics, scientific instruments, jet planes and engines, small computers, fine chemicals, and pharmaceuticals—in all of which human skill is the largest ingredient. Dr. Alexander Keynan, recent chairman of the National Council for Research and Development, says, "It has no limitation. There is no end to ideas." And Dayan adds, "Our main challenge is not whether we have better Hilton hotels but whether there is a job at the Weizmann Institute or the Hadassah Hospital."

In agriculture, Israel wants highly intensive "California-style" production, to become what Allon calls "the green house of snow-bound Europe." Here, the problem is water. The United States Government is helping to plan a $200 million nuclear-powered plant on the Mediterranean, probably at Ashdod, to desalt water and generate electricity. The planning has bogged down because desalting is still so expensive, but experts predict the Israelis will be doing a lot of desalting in the next 20 years. If there is peace, that means a plentiful supply of water for the whole region.

Even more urgent is Israel's surprising shortage of managerial skills. Productivity and quality control have suffered badly. Says David Horowitz, the governor of the Bank of Israel, "We have scientific know-how, but managerial know-how is rather limited. We didn't have many people experienced in the management of industry." Or as one economist says more informally, "In Israel, Jews have become good soccer players and poor chess players."

Israelis have never fostered private enterprise and are often suspicious of profit-making. Their Socialist economy is dominated by the bureaucracies of the government and the million-member Histadrut union, which not only plays a major role in the preeminent Israel Labor party but itself owns industries producing 20 percent of the country's GNP. One in every four employees works for Histadrut. And because the country was built on an egalitarian philosophy, under which all men are economically equal, wage differentials are very small. Incentives have been discouraged. Limits on opportunity are one prime reason why 150,000 Israelis have emigrated in the past 20 years and about 1,000 still leave every month.

The Israelis are trying to change all this. Histadrut now recognizes the need for incentives, private enterprise, and economic growth. Since capital from abroad, which made up 30 percent of Israel's total resources in 1950, has shrunk to eight percent, more and more, Israel will have to go it alone. Private investment is being stimulated by liberal new tax laws. In the years ahead, Socialist ideology will wither, and Israel hopes 20 years from now to be a center of industry and research. Says U.S. economist Robert Nathan, "Israel in the next 20 years will be a big exporter of brains to developing countries."

Even if the country can attract capital and skills, it still has another major problem: markets. The closest ones, in the Arab countries, are sealed off, and even if there were peace, it would be a long time before the poor Arabs could afford many of Israel's complex goods. The best markets are in

Western Europe and the United States. Israel has been seeking associate membership in the Common Market. "For us, it's absolutely essential," says banker Horowitz.

Today, Israel is not economically viable. Its leaders know this and are straining to do something about it. The younger generation of politicians especially wants to throw out the old Socialist dogmas and stimulate competition and efficiency. It's a hard job. But Israel has the brainpower and they will to pull it off. Given peace.

4. Integrating the Society. In 20 years, Israel has absorbed 1.2 million immigrants, nearly double its original Jewish population. Most have been penniless, unskilled, Sephardic refugees from the Muslim countries in Africa and Asia, the so-called "Orientals." Their customs are vastly different from those of the European-born original settlers. They are at the bottom of the economic scale and feel discriminated against. Says Dr. Israel Katz, director of The Hebrew University School of Social Work, "The gap has increased between these two groups and is increasing right now."

The Orientals now make up more than half the population. While 60 percent of the elementary school population come from this Oriental majority, only 13 percent of the Jews in Israel's colleges and universities do. As far as it has gone, integrating these newcomers into the society has been a phenomenal achievement, but it is still the nation's toughest internal, unfinished business. Prime Minister Eshkol says, "I believed once it would take ten years. It was a mistake. It looks like you need another 20 years."

Before the war last June, European-born Jews feared that the Orientals had dangerously diluted the old team spirit that saw the nation safely through the wars of 1948 and 1956. But the sons of Oriental Jews fought for their new country as vigorously and bravely as did the Western-descended Sabras. Now, the old-timers talk proudly of the entire younger generation.

Of course, over the months, the postwar euphoria of unity has slowly faded. Competition for jobs, concern about whom one's daughter might marry, resentment over special privileges for the more-deprived Orientals have reasserted themselves. But there is hope that the pre-June prejudices are diminishing. If Israel is to become truly one society, they will have to be overcome.

The schools and the army are dedicated to closing the division. But educational funds are short, and, says Dr. Judith T. Shuval of the Israel Institute of Applied Social Research, "The school system is structured to prevent mobility of underprivileged children through it. It is a system that is geared to an elite . . . It filters out the kids the system should be more interested in helping."

Many older Israelis still fear that the newcomers, with less drive for material gains, will convert Israel into "a Levantine state," with corruption, laziness, and self-interest above all. But Dr. Louis Miller, Director of Mental Health of the Ministry of Health, believes the newcomers' feeling for human relationships may even save the society, "Their drives are not so monopolistic. Whether they wish to or not, they will contribute to a modification of our society. This doesn't mean reduced efficiency. It means increased efficiency. Western civilization may break on the point of human relations."

Israel's future depends greatly on how well the various elements in the society can learn to work and live together without the pressure of war. Says one high official, "The challenges of peace may be greater than those of war."

5. THE JEWISH STATE. Since the June war, a new concern has come stage center in Israeli minds: the Arabs inside. Before the war, the Arabs were a minority of less than 400,000, usually segregated, not allowed to serve in the armed forces, and despite their resentments, not much worry to anyone. Over the years, there have even been 3,000 marriages be-

tween Jews and Arabs, always a Jewish girl and an Arab boy, and in every case, reportedly, the girl adopted Islam.

But the war left Israel with perhaps a million Arabs, and whatever border agreements may be worked out, a lot of Arabs will stay in Israel. Since their birthrate is much higher than that of the Jews, in time, Arabs may have a majority in the country. If Israel retains its strong belief in democracy, the Arabs could run the country.

To most Israelis, this is a threat; they don't want to be a minority again. They believe deeply that the future Israel must remain a Jewish state, with Hebrew its language and the Old Testament at the center of its culture. Otherwise, they say, Israel has neither safety nor meaning. Abba Eban says, "We do not want to be swamped by non-Hebrew culture. The majority feeling would not be in favor of threatening the Jewish character of our state."

This problem raises practical political questions: Should the Arabs on the West Bank be retained or returned to Jordan, or even made a separate nation? If they are kept, should they be second-class citizens, without political rights? Or should the Jews accept change and modify their own vision of their society? Most Israelis would prefer to get rid of their newly acquired Arabs.

A few Israelis want to hold on to what they call a Greater Israel. Aharon Amir, a Tel Aviv publisher, says, "I believe Israel is a nation in the making—the modern parallel of the American phenomenon. First it is a nation, not a religious community. The integration of the Arabs is a step toward Israel's greatness. Not to remain exclusive—that's the main thing." He predicts that if Israel returns the newly conquered territories, the Arabs will decide that they have nothing to lose by attacking again. "Then Israel is doomed in 20 or 30 years."

The Arabs are forcing the Israelis to think about their Jewishness. Less than one-third of Israeli Jews are actively religious. "The war was no ordinary thing. It's a chapter to be attached to the Bible," says Chief Rabbi Isar Yehuda Unterman. And Dr. Yaacov Herzog adds, "The Sabra is beginning to ask: 'Who am I?' "

Dr. S. N. Eisenstadt, professor of sociology at The Hebrew University, takes a different view: "I don't think people have become more religious. The religious groups have become more aggressive. They have tried to cash in on the war as the custodians of God, and this was such a great miracle."

But even Moshe Dayan, who grew up in the Socialist kibbutz tradition, now says: "If we have a majority or almost a majority of Arabs, it will remain a state in the Middle East but would not be the state of the Jewish people . . . I want the Jewish state to stay Jewish. We are part and parcel of the Jewish people. I am first Moshe, not General Dayan. I am a Jew first and an Israeli second. There is no conflict between the two. If there were a conflict, that would be a benefit for the Jewish people and not so good for the state of Israel; I would vote for the good of the Jewish people."

As the able political leader Shimon Peres says, "Every man carries in his heart a responsibility to his fathers."

Unlike pluralistic America, where several protestant variants of Judaism coexist, Israel has only orthodoxy. And the Chief Rabbinate is protected by the minority religious parties, which have joined the governing coalition in exchange for control over births, marriages, burials, food, and even traffic on the Sabbath. When the younger political leaders—like Dayan, Peres and Kollek—achieve the electoral reforms they demand, the power of the religious parties will be cut. Professor of Philosophy Nathan Rotenstreich, rector of The Hebrew University, believes the failure to achieve a new religious orientation is "a major shortcoming of Israel." Rabbi Moshe Davis, American-born head of the Institute of Contemporary Jewry at The Hebrew University, agrees, "In Israel, there is a tug-of-war between traditions, and there is no question that what will emerge is a modernized tradition . . . Within the next 20 years, Israel . . . will be the one place in the world where Jewish values and Jewish ideas will have a natural evolution and will have every chance of developing naturally."

6. The Jews Abroad. Israel cannot survive the next 20 years without help from Jews abroad. It needs not only cultural and financial support but immigrants. Finance Minister Sapir says, "During the next 20 years, we have to be 4.5 to 5.5 million Jews and another million minorities." Births will only supply one million of this increase; the rest must come from immigration. Says Dr. Herzog, "We crucially need immigration to develop a technological society."

For years, Israel's leaders preached that all good Jews should come to live there. They no longer expect this kind of Exodus. They recognize that Jews in the West are not coming in any numbers and want them to retain their religious identity in their own countries. At the same time, they are trying to attract immigrants by giving them employment, housing, and "the feeling that they're wanted."

Now that 97 percent of the Jews who lived in Arab countries have left and only 250,000 Jews remain in Communist Eastern Europe, Israelis hope that the Soviet Union will permit much of its three million Jewish population to emigrate to Israel. At present, there is no chance of this. But Eshkol is hopeful, "It may take another 50 years, but we'll have Jews from Russia. Before the Six Day War, we were already getting 2,000 per annum."

David Ben-Gurion, long the strongest advocate of American Jews' coming to Israel, now says, "A lot depends on American Jewry. Will they come? I think one, two percent will come. This is vitally important. We need more people, more science, more initiative."

He adds thoughtfully: "I don't believe all Jews will settle in Israel. I would like that they should remain Jews." Dayan proposes to offer every Jew who wants one an Israeli passport. "We are the only address he can apply to. I would enjoy doing it," he says.

"We want to live as every nation," says Education Minister Zalman Aranne. "Nobody wants to disappear. A world that will accept the crucifixion of the Jewish people isn't worth having. I don't see why we must disappear."

Israel's future is still perilous. Besieged, Israel cannot survive without friends—Jews and non-Jews. Open to the persecuted, it must still fuse one people out of many. Immature, it must find the meaning of being "a Jewish state," as it approaches the third millennium after Christ.

In Jerusalem, I spent one afternoon talking with a group of students at The Hebrew University. To these young people, Zionism is an anachronism; they are Israelis because they are there. They have no memories of pogroms and persecutions. Said one girl, "We think of Zionism in quotes, and we smile at the old songs they sing. They were all right for 50 years ago." These young people will have to battle out their own meaning of Israel.

They will also, it seems inevitable, continue to search for a Jewish identity rooted in the Western Wall, the Dead Sea Scrolls, and the Bible. They will decide, by the lives they lead, whether Jewishness is to be preserved, not out of stubbornness now but out of merit. They will determine whether being Jewish will have any meaning beyond being an Israeli. If not, the Western Wall will become just another historical tourist attraction, perhaps like the Roman Forum. If it has some deeper meaning for the future, then they may build a strong, secure nation where democracy and tolerance and a sense of helping others will override the noisy, jostling vibrancy of Tel Aviv.

When I asked David Ben-Gurion about Israel's future, he smiled and said that prophecy is a dangerous business in his country; there is too much competition. And that is true.

From Isaiah to Ben-Gurion himself, prophets have walked this land.

But the choice before this rugged, determined ministate is clear. One thoughtful Israeli says, "Is Israel going to be the David who beat Goliath or the David who wrote the Psalms? That's the real issue now. Facing us now is this challenge." For the next 20 years, at least, Israel will have to be both.